The Game Jam Survival Guide

Build a game in one crazy weekend and survive to tell the tale!

Christer Kaitila

PUBLISHING

BIRMINGHAM - MUMBAI

The Game Jam Survival Guide

Copyright © 2012 Packt Publishing

First published: April 2012

Production Reference: 1200312

Published by Packt Publishing Ltd.
Livery Place
35 Livery Street
Birmingham B3 2PB, UK.

ISBN 978-1-849692-50-2

www.packtpub.com

Cover Image by Asher Wishkerman (a.wishkerman@mpic.de)

Credits

Author
Christer Kaitila

Reviewer
Joseph Labrecque

Acquisition Editor
Joanna Finchen

Technical Editor
Aaron Rosario

Proofreader
Dan McMahon

Indexer
Monica Ajmera Mehta

Production Coordinator
Arvindkumar Gupta

Cover Work
Arvindkumar Gupta

About the Author

 The author of this book, **Christer Kaitila**, B.Sc. is a veteran video game developer with 17 years of professional experience. A hardcore gamer, dad, dungeon master, artist, and musician, he never takes himself too seriously and loves what he does for a living: making games!

A child of the arcade scene, he programmed his first videogame in the eighties, long before the Internet or hard drives existed. The first programming language he ever learned was 6809 assembly language, followed by BASIC, Turbo Pascal, VB, C++, Lingo, PHP, JavaScript, and finally ActionScript. He grew up as an elite BBS sysop in the MS-DOS era and was an active member of the demoscene in his teens. He put himself through university by providing freelance software programming services for clients. Since then, he has been an active member of the indie game development community and is known by his fellow indies as Breakdance McFunkypants.

Christer frequently joins Game Jams to keep his skills sharp. Over the years, he has programmed puzzle games, multiplayer RPGs, action titles, shooters, racing games, chat-rooms, persistent online worlds, browser games, and many business applications for clients ranging from 3D displays for industrial devices to simulations made for engineers.

He is the author of the book *Adobe Flash 11 Stage3D (Molehill) Game Programming Beginner's Guide* (`https://www.packtpub.com/adobe-flash11-stage3d-molehill-game-programming-beginners-guide/book`). He is one of the administrators of Ludum Dare (`http://www.ludumdare.com/compo/`) and has hosted a mini weekend Jam (`http://www.ludumdare.com/compo/2011/06/05/ready-for-the-june-minild/`) with the theme of "all talk: dialogue and conversation". He also created the keynote lecture for Ludum Dare 21 (`http://www.youtube.com/watch?v=aHD1QBP4ww8`), an eight minute video filled with words of encouragement and advice.

His client work portfolio is available at `www.orangeview.net` and his personal game development blog is `www.mcfunkypants.com`, where you can read more about the indie game community and his recent projects.

He lives in Victoria, Canada with his beloved wife, and the cutest baby son you've ever seen.

About the Contributors

Many people helped to make this book possible. It was a true community effort. The support, encouragement, and enthusiasm of the Game Jam community toward this book was a humbling (and wonderful) experience.

Peppered throughout the book in "what the experts say" sections are excerpts of interviews that were conducted as part of the research.

It is with deep respect and thanks that the following people appear in this book:

Mike "PoV" Kasprzak (Ludum Dare administrator)

Ian Schreiber (organizer of the Global Game Jam)

Chevy Ray Johnston (author of the *FlashPunk* engine)

Jason P. Kaplan (founder of the Game Prototype Challenge)

Pekka "pekuja" Kujansuu (Ludum Dare administrator)

Austin Breed (organizer of the Newgrounds Game Jams)

Christopher "Jack" Nilssen (independent game developer)

Phil Hassey (Ludum Dare administrator)

Chris "fydo" Hopp (Ludum Dare administrator)

Zuraida Buter (organizer of the Global Game Jam)

Mike "Hamumu" Hommel (Ludum Dare administrator)

Foaad Khosmood (director of the Global Game Jam)

Eric McQuiggan (founding member of *The Dirty Rectangles*)

Dr. Mike Reddy (organizer of the Global Game Jam)

And many others.

About the Reviewer

Joseph Labrecque is primarily employed by the University of Denver as senior interactive software engineer specializing in the Adobe Flash Platform, where he produces innovative academic toolsets for both traditional desktop environments and emerging mobile spaces. Alongside this principal role, he often serves as adjunct faculty, communicating upon a variety of Flash platform solutions and general web design and development subjects.

In addition to his accomplishments in higher education, Joseph is the proprietor of Fractured Vision Media, LLC—a digital media production company, technical consultancy, and distribution vehicle for his creative works. He is founder and sole abiding member of the dark ambient recording project *An Early Morning Letter, Displaced* whose releases have received international award nominations and underground acclaim.

Joseph has contributed to a number of respected community publications as an article writer and video tutorialist and is author of books such as *Flash Development for Android Cookbook* (2011 Packt Publishing—ISBN: 1849691428), *What's New in Adobe AIR 3* (2011 O'Reilly Media—ISBN: 9781449311070), *What's New in Flash Player 11* (2011 O'Reilly Media—ISBN: 9781449311094), and is a co-author of *Mobile Development with Flash Professional CS5.5* and *Flash Builder 4.5: Learn by Video* (2011 Adobe Press—ISBN: 0321788109).

He regularly speaks at user group meetings and industry conferences such as Adobe MAX, FITC, D2W, 360|Flex, and a variety of other educational and technical conferences. In 2010, he received an Adobe Impact Award in recognition of his outstanding contribution to the education community. He has served as an Adobe Education Leader since 2008 and is also an Adobe Community Professional.

www.PacktPub.com

Support files, eBooks, discount offers and more

You might want to visit www.PacktPub.com for support files and downloads related to your book.

Did you know that Packt offers eBook versions of every book published, with PDF and ePub files available? You can upgrade to the eBook version at www.PacktPub.com and as a print book customer, you are entitled to a discount on the eBook copy. Get in touch with us at service@packtpub.com for more details.

At www.PacktPub.com, you can also read a collection of free technical articles, sign up for a range of free newsletters and receive exclusive discounts and offers on Packt books and eBooks.

http://PacktLib.PacktPub.com

Do you need instant solutions to your IT questions? PacktLib is Packt's online digital book library. Here, you can access, read and search across Packt's entire library of books.

Why Subscribe?

- Fully searchable across every book published by Packt
- Copy and paste, print and bookmark content
- On demand and accessible via web browser

Free Access for Packt account holders

If you have an account with Packt at www.PacktPub.com, you can use this to access PacktLib today and view nine entirely free books. Simply use your login credentials for immediate access.

Table of Contents

Preface

The TouchArcade Game Jam

What is a Game Jam?

Game Jams are fun. They are a creative, exciting, social experience. The goal of a Game Jam is to design a video game, either alone or in teams, as fast as humanly possible; usually in a single weekend. Some Jams are also great for making board games or card games!

Game Jams can be absolutely massive group events held in conference rooms and computer labs, or can be intimate affairs taking place in a friend's living room. Others are online-only events where people work on games at the same time in their own homes and share the results at a website.

The key ingredient in a Game Jam is time pressure. Whether spanning a 48-hour weekend, an entire week, or just a few hours, the essential attribute shared by all Jams is a limited time-frame. The deadline forces participants to speed-code. To cut corners. To think outside the box, and to whip something up as fast as they can.

Almost all Game Jams focus around a theme. This theme is often a closely guarded secret until the Jam begins, and participants are challenged to come up with a fitting game idea.

Occasionally, Jams have a competitive element: each entry is voted upon and a winner is declared.

Whether there is voting or not, Game Jams aren't really about winning or losing: they are community-run, highly social, feel-good events full of camaraderie from your game developer peers.

Whatever the format or rules, the goal of a Game Jam is to create your very own game as quickly as possible. Some rise to the challenge and finish amazing feats of programming. Many more fail brilliantly and never get to the finish line. Regardless of the outcome, everyone has fun. That's the whole point of a Game Jam.

The goal of this book

This book has a mission statement: build an amazing game that you're proud of and will entertain players, all in one crazy 48-hour Game Jam weekend—and survive to tell the tale!

Embrace the best practices and techniques of past Game Jam winners and avoid common pitfalls along the way to the finish line. You too can survive a 48-hour game development marathon with your mind intact and an amazing game to show off to friends and family!

With this book you will learn the secret techniques that master Game Jammers use to create winning entries. We'll start by exploring great ways to brainstorm and design a game based on a given theme. We'll discover the best tools and techniques to finish a game in a weekend of coding, with anecdotes and advice from past winners and losers combined with humorous words of encouragement which are sure to help you on your way. Finally, this book will present a list of Game Jams around the world, online communities worth checking out, and fantastic engines, art resources and people worth discovering.

If you follow the system shared in this book, you will be able to build an amazing game in a single weekend—regardless of your programming or game design experience.

What this book covers

Chapter 1, Before the Jam: Prepare Yourself for Success! — We begin with a positive and enthusiastic look at the mindset required for achieving success. Learn about finding creative freedom in constraints, preparing base code and art tools, forming a team, and using social networking. Discover the behaviors that you will want to avoid. This book features an infographic from a questionnaire answered by over 700 Game Jammers. It includes interviews with **Ian Schreiber** (organizer of the Global Game Jam), **Eric McQuiggan** (founding member of The Dirty Rectangles), **Jason P. Kaplan** (founder of the Game Prototype Challenge), plus **Mike "PoV" Kasprzak** and **Mike "Hamumu" Hommel** (Ludum Dare administrators).

Chapter 2, Hours 1-12: Your Quest Begins! — How to hit the ground running, reduce stress, and deal with the theme. Learn from the mistakes of others through an analysis of postmortem ("What went right? What went wrong?") blog posts and articles, presented in infographic form. Features interviews with **Chevy Ray Johnston** (author of the FlashPunk game engine and winner of multiple Ludum Dares) and **Dr. Mike Reddy** (organizer of the Global Game Jam). You will learn how to come up with a great plan, the best ways to design your game, and techniques for brainstorming.

Chapter 3, Hours 13-24: Deeper into the Jungle! — Learn how to stay motivated by always moving forward through the use of placeholder art and design simplification. Features an interview with **Austin Breed** (founder of the Newgrounds Game Jams). Find essential mechanics so that you can finish a playable prototype early, with time left over for polishing and play-testing.

Chapter 4, Hours 25-36: Breaking Through The Wall! — The late stages of any project are always the most difficult. Discover techniques for working around bugs, dealing with stress, and keeping morale high. Includes a discussion of time management, code simplification, automation of art assets, iterative development, and when to break the rules of computer science. Includes an interview with **Christopher "DarkAcreJack" Nilsson**. From Occam's Razor to Brook's Law, we focus on common mistakes, ways to reduce production time, and dealing with imperfection.

Chapter 5, Hours 37-48: Getting to the Finish Line! — As the light at the end of the tunnel approaches, the really fun part begins. Learn techniques to finish on time and with your sanity intact. Deal with unforeseen hassles, tie up loose ends, trim the fat and polish polish polish. An exploration of the common features of winning games is also included. Featuring interviews with **Pekka "pekuja" Kujansuu** (Ludum Dare administrator) and **Foaad Khosmood** (director of the Global Game Jam). Learn what to do when you're in danger of missing the deadline, and how to package and submit your game. Focus on the importance of the name, description, and icon, as well as control schemes, difficulty balance and ways to "hook" the player.

Chapter 6, After the Jam: Fame and Fortune! – Congratulations! You did it. Now what? A discussion of all the ancillary activities you can perform after the Jam, such as playing and voting on games by your fellow developers, writing a post-mortem analysis, preparing the game for a public (commercial) release, attracting sponsorship or advertisers and getting your game on app stores and portals. Features interviews from **Chris "fydo" Hopp** and **Phil Hassey** (Ludum Dare administrators).

Appendix A, Game Jams – A large listing of Game Jams around the world, with descriptions and website addresses.

Appendix B, Game Engines – A list of game engines that are frequently used by successful Game Jammers that includes information regarding what platforms they support and where to get them.

Appendix C, Helpful Tools – A list of handy tools to make your Game Jam more fun. Includes screen recorders (for creating time-lapse videos of your work), IRC clients, tools that help you generate sound effects, and popular level editors that work with common game engines.

Appendix D, The Community – A list of online resources to help you connect with your Game Jamming peers. Includes social networking links, active Twitter hashtags, enthusiast websites and blogs, IRC chatrooms, and community discussion forums worth visiting.

How to use this book

This survival guide is split into several chapters, each of which represents a particular time period in and around a typical 48-hour Game Jam. The first chapter covers your preparation before the Jam begins, and each subsequent chapter dives deeper into the experience, twelve hours at a time. The final chapter explores the possibilities beyond that initial weekend session.

Think of this book as a chronological journey from preparation through to the completion of a Game Jam project.

More important than generic advice, the purpose of this book is to provide specific, explicit bits of advice that you can follow to help you get to the finish line. You don't just want abstract advice such as "know your tools", you want specifics, such as "square grids are easier to program than hexagon grids".

In this book, you will find a number of styles of text that distinguish between different kinds of information. Here are some examples of these styles, and an explanation of their meaning.

New terms and **important words** are shown in bold.

 Warnings or important notes appear in a box like this.

Scattered throughout the book you can expect to find tips and tricks in with concrete examples of the kind of decision making required to finish a game in a short timeframe. Here's an example:

 Tips-n-Tricks: "First KISS"
Follow the K.I.S.S. rule: Keep It Simple, Stupid!

The author of this book is a veteran Game Jammer, but to get a better picture of the do's and don'ts of Jamming, the community was interrogated over a span of several months. Blog posts, Twitter questions, mailing list e-mails, and Google+ comments were collected. Questionnaires were sent out to the most influential and successful Game Jammers, and their answers and contributions appear throughout this book.

Just for fun, respondents on the "gamecompo" mailing list and Ludum Dare website were asked to write haiku (three line poems) that relate to achieving Game Jam success. These appear throughout the book and are meant to keep you on track with a little Jamming philosophy. Light-hearted little thoughts like the following:

 Haiku Time:
Even my best game, however much I polish, has programmer art.
— *Mikhail Rudoy*

Meet the two Jamming friends

Finally, we would like to introduce you to two fictional characters who will accompany us on our journey; a wise and humble baby, and a cocky loud-mouth puppet.

Because we don't want to put down any real people or use them as example of what not to do, using two fictional characters seemed like a wise way to avoid hurting anyone's feelings.

The first character is **Baby McFunkypants**, Game Jammer extraordinaire, and believer in keeping things simple. His games are small, he always finishes on time, and he has a fun time Jamming every weekend. In this book, he will give examples of "pro style".

The second is a puppet named **Lee Taxxor** who often finds himself in trouble due to being overly optimistic. He thinks he is an "elite hacker". He bites off more than he can chew and has yet to successfully complete a Game Jam. In this book, he will give examples of a "noob mistake".

Together, these two characters will help us compare and contrast game design philosophies from two opposing perspectives. What not to do, followed by an alternative more likely to lead to success.

Reader feedback

Feedback from our readers is always welcome. Let us know what you think about this book—what you liked or may have disliked. Reader feedback is important for us to develop titles that you really get the most out of.

To send us general feedback, simply send an e-mail to feedback@packtpub.com, and mention the book title in the subject of your message.

If there is a topic that you have expertise in and you are interested in either writing or contributing to a book, see our author guide on www.packtpub.com/authors.

Customer support

Now that you are the proud owner of a Packt book, we have a number of things to help you to get the most from your purchase.

Errata

Although we have taken every care to ensure the accuracy of our content, mistakes do happen. If you find a mistake in one of our books—maybe a mistake in the text or the code—we would be grateful if you would report this to us. By doing so, you can save other readers from frustration and help us improve subsequent versions of this book. If you find any errata, please report them by visiting http://www.packtpub.com/support, selecting your book, clicking on the **errata submission form** link, and entering the details of your errata. Once your errata are verified, your submission will be accepted and the errata will be uploaded to our website, or added to any list of existing errata, under the Errata section of that title.

Piracy

Piracy of copyright material on the Internet is an ongoing problem across all media. At Packt, we take the protection of our copyright and licenses very seriously. If you come across any illegal copies of our works, in any form, on the Internet, please provide us with the location address or website name immediately so that we can pursue a remedy.

Please contact us at copyright@packtpub.com with a link to the suspected pirated material.

We appreciate your help in protecting our authors, and our ability to bring you valuable content.

Questions

You can contact us at questions@packtpub.com if you are having a problem with any aspect of the book, and we will do our best to address it.

The Protoplay Game Jam

What the experts say: *Zuraida Buter*

The best thing about Game Jams is being together and meeting new people that are spending 48 hours in one location, passionately creating games.

I hope that in the future, Game Jams will blow our brains out with the most creative, experimental and crazy games ever made (oh, and that female participants > 40%).

To me, Jamming is all about it being a fun spirited event about people and games where passion meets creativity, sharing, and collaboration.

It is always fantastic to see the excitement build up, culminating in an explosion of Jam happiness and fantastic games.

 **Zuraida Buter** is one of the Global Game Jam Directors, initiated Indigo (a showcase for Dutch indie games), organized several Game Jams throughout the years and is passionate advocate for collaboration and indie game devs.

Website: http://www.zo-ii.com

Twitter: http://twitter.com/zoewi

Google+: https://plus.google.com/113482563586225259866/

1

Before the Jam: Prepare Yourself for Success!

"The enemy of art is the absence of limitations"

-Orson Welles

You CAN do it!

With a little positivity and a lot of hard work, you will succeed. There are several techniques listed in this book that will give you an edge over your competitors.

The IndieArcade Game Jam

This chapter will cover the things that you should do before the Jam, such as:

- Preparing your tools
- Forming a team
- Social networking
- Things to avoid
- Preparing for success

Finding freedom in constraints

Creativity flows when it is constrained, whereas unbridled freedom is strangely inhibiting. The famous quote by Orson Welles above conveys this perfectly. Another example to illustrate this theory is Norman Rockwell's paintings.

When he was given a limitation of only black and red ink for his first magazine cover commission (http://bit.ly/zH4hNN), he worked within these constraints and developed a signature art style that launched his career. Would he have become so famous if allowed to use any other colors?

Creative constraints can give rise to surprising new ideas and can also improve the design of your game. For example, statistics were collected during an analysis of the **Ludum Dare** Game Jam's "post-mortem" blog entries in which Jammers listed "what went right" and "what went wrong" while making their game. A significant percentage of jammers reported being very happy with their art when they used a limited palette of colors, and conversely, a significant percentage were unhappy with their art when they used all the colors of the rainbow. Sepia-toned, subtle, complementing color choices are just one example of how imposing creative limits on yourself may in fact improve the final product.

The major creative constraint that Game Jams provide is time. Some game developers take up to five years to produce a single game. Many AAA console games took several hundred human-years of labor if you consider the time and number of people working on them.

When faced with the frenetic pace required to make a game from scratch on a single weekend, it will take creativity and some "out of the box" thinking to get to the finish line. Along the way, you might just find that your ideas are fresher and more inspired because these constraints push you outside your comfort zone.

Feeling excited enough to dive in and make a game in 48 hours? Your first step is to choose an event and sign up. The most popular and longest running Jams are listed in the *Appendix 1, Game Jams.*

What the experts say: *Eric McQuiggan*

Some big things that I find work well in the many Game Jams that I've been a part of or organized:

Centralized location: This is important as it allows people to get together and bounce ideas off of each other. It also helps teams get together and games get finished.

Rigid and adhered-to rules (to a point): As with most creative endeavors, the more stringent the situation, the more the creativity comes through (most of the time anyway). There is nothing more intimidating than a blank slate.

Some constrictions could be *Time* (48 hours is good, one week is alright), *Palette*, *Screen Size*, or *Theme* (most important).

Don't try out new tools: It's hard enough to make a game in a tiny timeframe, but when you compound that with having to learn a new skill set, it makes things really difficult.

Sleep: People think they can skip it, but it really makes your last day of the Jam terrible.

Eric McQuiggan is a founding member of The Dirty Rectangles which has held various Game Jams, makes Flash games at Fuel Industries and is Vice President of the Ottawa Chapter of the IGDA.

Website: http://ericmcquiggan.com/
Dirty Rectangles: http://www.dirty-rectangles.com/
Twitter: http://twitter.com/EricMcQuiggan
Google+: https://plus.google.com/107925618193899227412

Game Jam survey stats

In December 2011, participants of Ludum Dare 22 were asked to fill out a survey on their experience. Ludum Dare is a 48-hour Game Jam, and over 2000 participants joined in the fun where a total of 891 games were completed. 747 people filled out the survey. Here are the results:

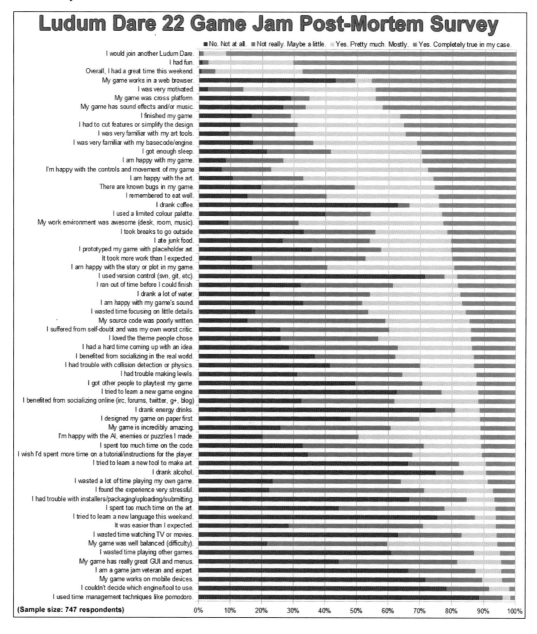

Looking at the stats in the previous image gives a pretty clear picture of what it is like to join a Game Jam. Most importantly, people have a lot of fun.

A majority of participants were either first-timers or less experienced Game Jammers. Most are happy with their games, of which about half work in a web browser. In order to finish on time, many people had to cut features and simplify their designs. Not everyone was as familiar with their tools or **base code** (source code that is the starting point for the game) as they should have been, and only a few tried to learn a brand new engine.

Most games did not run on mobile devices, but many were cross-platform. On average, most people did not spend time watching TV or movies, going outside, visiting friends, or playing other games.

Contrary to expectations, almost nobody drank coffee, energy drinks, or alcohol. Virtually nobody used **version control** (such as SVN or GIT) or time-management techniques (such as `http://en.wikipedia.org/wiki/Pomodoro_Technique`). Surprisingly, not many reported having difficulty with packaging, installers, or submitting.

Perhaps the most telling statistic from the survey is that nearly everyone who participated plans to do so again. Game Jamming is fun, and addictive!

What the experts say: *Jason P. Kaplan*

The best thing about Game Jams is making something new and, hopefully, unique. With full-sized projects, one feels the need to be profitable, safe, and so on, which leads to familiar and iterative games. With Jams where there's nothing on the line but a day or a week of work, we find ourselves willing to break down walls and try new things.

If I could give one piece of advice to newcomers, it would be: Master your technology. Don't go into a Jam thinking you'll make a brilliant game on a new tech that you haven't used before. Know everything about the engine that you're coding in, your art tools, and your skill set. Only learn new things when you have copious time to afford said learning.

Jason P. Kaplan is the founder and organizer of the Game Prototype Challenge, and a game developer and designer. Passionate about helping people to get motivated and make games, he tries to distil said motivation to make his own games.

Website: `http://jpkgames.com`

Game Jam: `http://gameprototypechallenge.com`

Twitter: `http://twitter.com/jasonpkaplan`

Go with what you know

If you start from scratch or use a game engine that you've never tried before over the Game Jam weekend, it is highly unlikely that you'll finish anything more than a tech demo by the end. The learning curve is simply too steep. You'll spend all your time learning the new technology.

For this reason, the wise Jammer already has a game engine picked out, installed, and ready to go before the Jam begins. Now is not the time to try to learn a brand new engine. Get to know it before the Jam.

There is a list of popular game engines in *Appendix 1, Game Jams*.

Preparing your base code

The prepared warrior is sure to win in battle. It is not enough to have a game engine picked out. If you really want to make the best use of your limited time, you would be well served by first preparing a **base code** project.

What is "base code"?

More than just a game engine, a base code project is one that is already set up and ready to compile and run. A game engine downloaded from the web can take hours or even days to get set up and ready for use. Finding dependencies, installing plugins, fixing file paths for included files, and ensuring that everything compiles are things that a prepared Jammer has already completed long before the Jam begins. This template project, sort of a "hello world" app, should be a working, albeit simplistic game. The best base code already has all the "wiring" done to enable features such as a title screen, simplistic game logic, scorekeeping, sounds, asset loading, initializing graphics, and more.

Instead of opening up your editor and starting with a blank project at the beginning of a Game Jam, truly having your tools at the ready, much like sharpening your sword long before entering a battle, will help you hit the ground running.

One way to save time before a Jam is to create base code template projects for archetypical game genres that you are interested in. For example: a platformer; a grid-based puzzle game; a top-view scrolling shoot-'em-up (bullet hell game); or a visual novel style adventure game.

Many Game Jams will allow you to start from a base code template if you "declare" it at the beginning of the competition. Declaring your base code could be as simple as providing a link on your "I'm in!" blog post, that would allow others to download the same base code if they wanted to use it as well. This keeps the playing field level, yet allows you to have a working skeleton game ready to be fleshed out.

Even before the Game Jam "theme" has been revealed, many participants already have a genre of game that they've decided to embrace. Pick something that you've always wanted to make and simply fit the theme into that genre as best you can. Just remember, some genres are more labor-intensive and complex than others!

  "I'm going to create a massively multiplayer, free-roam 3D RPG with realistic physics, vehicles, a deep crafting system with in-app-payments and live video chat!"

  "I like the KISS rule: Keep It Simple, Stupid! Since I only have two days I'm going to make a single-player 2D puzzle game with one or two levels."

What the experts say: *Mike Kasprzak*

There just isn't enough time to make something the "right" way. Instead, you need to pick the fastest way. Not the fastest-performing way, but the fastest way you can get things working. Your time is most precious. For me, this was an incredibly refreshing realization... Jamming is like going through an entire product development cycle in a fraction of the usual time. You can try something out, note what did or did not work, and try again straight away.

Pick something that will take you only a couple of hours to make, then stop thinking and go make it. Get it working as soon as possible. Use dummy art. I like to throw-down simple geometric shapes such as circles, squares, triangles, and pluses (N.B.: This is not a PlayStation ad). And once it works, polish and make it better until you run out of time.

A Jam is an incredible teaching tool. We hate to admit it, but some facets of the game industry are cruel and punishing, the crunch especially. The thing is, crunching isn't necessarily a bad thing, it's just how we typically use it in the game biz. Jamming is probably the best way to understand the good, the bad, and the ugly of the crunch before you decide to make it a career.

More often than not, crunching a Game Jam game is some of the purest and most fulfilling game development you'll ever do. You're creating something for you. When you're done, you'll have something to show and admire, and the time commitment was just a couple days instead of the months and years a typical game takes.

Mike "PoV" Kasprzak runs Sykhronics Entertainment and is one of the organizers behind Ludum Dare. He's the author of many games, including Smiles HD, a puzzle matching game that's currently available for nearly all mobile devices of today. Aside from being a finalist in the Independent Games Festival Mobile in 2009, Mike has won some pretty crazy prizes with Smiles including a Smart Car.

Blog: http://www.toonormal.com

Twitter: http://twitter.com/mikekasprzak

Google+: http://google.com/profiles/mikekasprzak

Preparing your art tools

In addition to your game engine and development environment, you will want to have your art tools at the ready. Nothing is more frustrating than finding that you need to download and install something after the Jam begins, so test out your tools beforehand.

In a survey of Game Jam post-mortems, participants listed unfamiliarity with the art generation tool as the number one thing that went wrong. More frequent than code bugs, more annoying than installation hassles, more constricting than running out of time, it is the art production step which is the most common roadblock on the way to finishing your game.

If you are making a 2D game, ensure that you are thoroughly familiar with the program (such as Photoshop, GIMP, or Inkscape) that you plan to use. Know ahead of time what size and file format your art should be in order to work well in your game engine. Do your textures need to be square and 'power-of-two' in size? Can you use the Alpha channel? Will using images that are too big cause your engine to render poorly (or not at all)? Test out the process before the Jam. Make a sprite and get it working in your game engine.

The same holds true for 3D art; not only should you know how to sculpt a 3D mesh using 3ds Max, Blender, Sketchup, or Maya; but you need to be familiar with the export process. Practice getting art from a creation tool into your game, because there are always technical hassles. File format woes; size restrictions, technical constraints, bugs in the exporter are some of the potential hurdles.

Even the audio content pipeline should be premeditated. Does your game engine require `.ogg` files, `.mp3` files, or `.wav` files? What sample rate should be used? These and more questions should be sorted out beforehand to avoid hassles later.

Practice makes perfect

The rule of thumb is to be sure that you have practiced using your entire art creation tool chain. You don't want to have to learn how to export a mesh after the Jam begins. Expect format woes or exporter bugs the first time round. One way to avoid these headaches during the Jam itself is to test your content creation pipeline beforehand.

Create a sample sprite or mesh, a tiny game level, and an example sound effect. Export them all in the proper formats. Embed or import this data into your game engine. Compile a simple "hello world" example game and ensure that your art appears perfectly. Test whether your animations run, your sounds are audible, and that the empty game prototype runs without errors.

If you can do all of the above, your game creation tools are ready for Jamming. A wise warrior knows that sharpening your sword before battle is smarter than trying to do it on your enemy's armor.

OrcaJam 2011 in Victoria, Canada

Forming a team

Some Game Jams, especially those held in person (at convention centers or computer labs) encourage teamwork. Others, such as Ludum Dare and most virtual Jams are usually solo efforts. It can be exciting and fulfilling to work together with a couple of other people to make a game.

One person may be the main coder while others work on art, sound, or level design at the same time. By joining forces, you will accomplish twice as much than what you would if you tried to do everything yourself. Network with the people around you at the beginning of the Jam and see if you can connect with anyone. This can be a great way to make new friends!

Social networking tips

Making a game is great, but doing it with friends is far better. The Game Jam subculture is a social scene. Jammers frequently use IRC chat rooms, email mailing lists, blogs, and discussion forums, and networking is of course constant. Using social networking is essential for making connections with your peers.

You don't want to be simply coding in a sandbox, unaware of what others in the Jam are doing. Instead, try asking for help with bugs that have you stumped: there is sure to be someone on that chat room or blog who has experienced the same problem. By the same token, offering to help others with their problems (or simply to play-test their game) will make you popular and appreciated. Helping others is always the best way to achieve social media success: it isn't what others can do for you, but what you can provide to others, that makes the difference between an obscure Game Jam entry, and one that everyone is talking about and playing.

There is a list of social networking resources such as Google+, Twitter, and IRC chat rooms, as well as useful applications that help you make time-lapse videos in the *Appendix 3, Helpful Tools*.

Things to avoid

Many 'gotchas' worth looking out for, including:
Not having your tools ready
Trying to learn a new language or API
Going without sleep
Not going outside or taking a break
Not eating properly

Many first time Jammers make the mistake of diving into programming before getting their tools in order. When a Jam begins, you should already be familiar with your compiler, editor, and language.

You should have already installed the tools that you need to program the game and create the art. The game engine that you want to use should have already been downloaded, and you should have already tried making a simple tech demo or "hello world" example.

This preparatory stage is essential, since 48 hours is not very much time. Stories of entire days lost due to broken tools, missing .dlls, and getting over the learning curve are legendary.

Many a Jammer has failed to produce a game because they spent an entire weekend learning how to use the game engine that they hoped to become familiar with.

  "This weekend sounds like the perfect time to learn something completely new, so I've just downloaded a wicked looking engine and brand new compiler that I'm going to use for the first time while working on my game!"

  "I want to spend the entire weekend working on my game and not waste the first day setting up my tools and getting over the learning curve, getting familiar with a framework that I've never used before, so I'm going to stick with what I know already. I have a simple game engine from a previous project that I'm going to start with and I'm using tools that I've had for years. I'm gonna stick with what I know so that I have a "hello world" app compiling without errors in the first 15 minutes."

Don't try a new language

Don't try to learn a completely new toolset or engine during the Jam, or that's all you will accomplish. In the same way that you wouldn't join a jazz music Jam with a musical instrument you've never touched before, once the Jam begins you should be using a tool that you are intimately familiar with. *Go with what you know*. If you are ever in doubt bout whether you should try the newest, latest, and greatest new tool, or a tool that you have already made a game or two with, the advice from the pros is "go with what you know". Now's not the time to do something for the first time.

Sleep is good

Another thing to avoid is attempting to go without sleep. Although there are stories of half crazed Jammers pulling multiple all-nighters and emerging from the sleepless fog with an award-winning masterpiece, the more common story is that of late night headaches, productivity dropping to near zero as fatigue kicks in, and *Monday morning misery*. Remember, you are most effective, faster, and quicker to fix bugs when you are fresh.

You will often come up with the solution to a tricky bug in your sleep. Your mind will mull over whatever it was that had you stumped the night before, so don't worry about getting a good night's sleep. The productivity gains that you will receive from taking short breaks, naps, and even getting your mind off the Jam for a walk outside are well worth the time spent away from your computer.

Real life matters

Quality of life matters, more so during a Game Jam. A little sunshine and some time spent with friends are going to help you have a fun weekend—and a life. Don't shackle yourself to your computer for the entire weekend. *Live a little*. Your game will be the better for it.

  "At the start of the weekend I'm gonna order one dozen pizzas, six bags of chips and two cases of beer. It is gonna be legendary!"

  "I find that my brain works best when I'm well hydrated. I'm going to drink tons of water, eat fruit and light, non-greasy food. This way I won't have a sugar crash or get headaches from caffeine withdrawal or a hangover."

Food = Brain Fuel

Another thing to avoid during a Jam is throwing your diet out the window. While many people will have a coffee or two when burning the midnight oil, as with all other things in life, moderation is the key. Too many beers, too much caffeine, or eating nothing but junk food will give you an initial burst of energy followed by a long hard crash or hangover. Your brain needs to be fuelled by *non-greasy foods* which tend to release energy over a longer period of time. Your thoughts will flow faster and clearer if you are well-hydrated—so *drink tons of water*. Always have a glass of juice or water by your computer. The better you treat yourself, the happier the entire experience will be.

Treating yourself well during a Jam doesn't just benefit you—your game will be better as well. You will create fewer inadvertent bugs if you are well rested and hydrated. Your morale will stay high if you aren't battling a pounding headache. Your mind will feel clear and swift, and your code will be masterful.

What the experts say: *Mike Hommel*

Don't be a stereotype. Red Bull and all-nighters is a surefire way to churn out garbage that crashes.

Don't skip on sleep, don't load up on caffeine. Just use normal waking hours and take breaks—go for a walk to clear your head, eat your food in front of the TV. Do these things to settle your brain down. If you're in a frenzy, you're gonna screw it all up, and you're going to burn out before the end. The end hours are the most important ones, you have to be at your best when you're looking at your game and deciding what kind of polish you can slap on in two more hours.

Keep a notebook. Then you can flip through that and consider it when the theme is announced. Another great thing to do is sit down and write out short phrases or sentences that the theme brings to mind. Does one of those expand into some kind of gameplay in your head? Look at every angle and every definition of the words. You might make the most creative game if you are the only one who realizes that "Gravity" can mean "somberness" as well as just "stuff falling down".

The genre or style of game that is most likely to win a Game Jam is "a surprise". If you make a plain old platformer, an RTS, or an FPS; that's not it. The genre of game that will win is "unique". Make something nobody has ever seen before. Invent some weird mechanic that nobody is expecting. If it's a flop, all you have lost is 48 hours!

Mike "Hamumu" Hommel is a successful indie game developer, the administrator of Ludum Dare, and one of the creators of nearly 50 games such as Robot Wants Kitty, Dr. Lunatic Supreme With Cheese, Kid Mystic, Loonyland, Mia's Happy Day, Sleepless Hollow, and more.

Website: http://hamumu.com

Twitter: http://twitter.com/hamumu

Google+: https://plus.google.com/101713959382687203463

Maintaining relationships

Surviving a Game Jam means more than just making it to the end with a finished game. It means more than simply staying alive during coding marathons. Truly surviving a Game Jam means that you also managed to maintain your real-world relationships.

Many Jammers have family responsibilities: shirk these and you know that you'll be suffering the consequences tenfold over the next few weeks. Instead of aiming to sleep in the doghouse for a month, take some time to spend with your family, fulfill your commitments, and show the people that you love exactly where they sit in your list of priorities (the very top).

Many wives and girlfriends (or husbands and boyfriends) may not take too kindly to your not being around to enjoy the weekend with them. It is imperative to get your loved ones on board with the whole idea. You can make up for the missing time by scheduling a special day trip or family outing on the day before the Jam (and perhaps also on the day after) to make up for it. Ego matters: if you put your wife in the credits as "executive producer" it **will** score you many bonus points.

Finally, get your social circle involved in the Game Jam itself: while taking a break for dinner, talk about game ideas and ask their opinions. Ask them for ideas. Ask them to be the beta-testers for your game. They'll feel like they were made part of the event.

Techniques to help you survive a Game Jam without getting a divorce

Booking the time well in advance so everyone knows it is coming up.

Making up for the time you're away: a family outing beforehand.

Putting your loved ones in the game credits.

Asking your kids for game ideas.

Getting your loved ones to provide voiceovers and sound effects.

Scanning your kid's artwork and use it for the game sprites.

Negotiating a way to make up for it: a date, chores, and so on.

Giving your partner weekend pass for something they love.

Getting your family to play the game you make afterwards.

Involving those you love in the Game Jam.

It only takes a little effort and caring to get your family and friends on board. This will avoid any guilt trips, bitterness, or feelings of neglect in the future. One tried-and-true technique is to book a family outing the day before a Game Jam. Talk about the fact that you'll be preoccupied over the next couple days and that the trip is meant to make up for it.

You will be able to enjoy the Jam that much more when you are unencumbered by feelings of guilt, so get your loved ones involved in the project. They will feel part of it rather than replaced by it.

What the experts say: *Ian Schreiber*

The best thing about Game Jams is they're a great equalizer: you can't tell the difference between a game made by amateurs and one made by pros most of the time.

If I could give one piece of advice to newcomers, it would be: don't be intimidated, just do it. You'll learn more in a weekend than you would in a year of classes.

Ian Schreiber is one of the organizers of the Global Game Jam. He has been in the gaming industry since the year 2000, first as a programmer and then as a game designer. He has taught game design and development courses at a variety of two-year and four-year colleges and universities, and has co-authored two books on games.

Blog: http://teachingdesign.blogspot.com/
Twitter: http://twitter.com/#!/ianschreiber

2
Hours 1-12:
Your Quest Begins!

"A student entered a Game Jam but was unable to complete anything of note. He turned to the developer beside him, whose game was lauded by all. "Master," the student exclaimed, "please teach me how to choose a path as you have. I considered a thousand game ideas, yet I could not decide the best one." "I wish I had your problems," the master sighed. "I only had one idea, so could not choose at all."

- Randommine

Hit the ground running!
Don't waste time with grand designs. Don't stress about the possibilities. Dive in head first and get started as quickly as you possibly can!

The Philly Game Jam

This chapter will focus on the early stages of a Game Jam. These most important first few hours will set the state for the rest of your experience. Topics that we will cover include:

- An analysis of past Game Jammer's experience
- Dealing with the Game Jam theme
- An example of a winning entry
- Coming up with a plan of action
- Brainstorming and prototyping

Learn from others' mistakes

As part of the research for this book, an in-depth analysis of blog posts tagged as post-mortem reports on the Ludum Dare website was performed. These post-mortems, as they are called, relate the experiences of each Jammer and are typically written just after their game has been submitted.

Game post-mortems typically include the following sections: an intro, in which the game itself is described, followed by "what went right" and "what went wrong" sections. They are most often posted on the author's blog, or on game development websites such as `www.gamasutra.com`. These reports contain a wealth of wisdom. The past experience of your peers is always a valuable source of information.

You can read hundreds of post-mortem reports here at
`http://www.ludumdare.com/compo/tag/postmortem/`

Another great list of game post-mortems can be found at
`http://www.pixelprospector.com/the-big-list-of-postmortems/`

Some of these statistics may surprise you, while others will merely confirm your gut instinct.

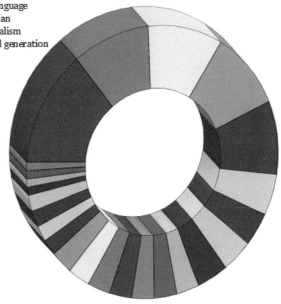

What went right?

Common statements from Ludum Dare game jam "post-mortem" reports 2010-2011

- familiarity with code base / framework / engine / language
- dealing with the theme / coming up with an idea / plan
- simplified the design / cut features / k.i.s.s. / minimalism
- good level editor / in game editor / procedural level generation
- happy with the sound/music
- happy with the art
- good art tools
- prototyping with placeholder graphics
- socializing / irc / chat / real life
- high motivation
- prototyping with real/final art
- limited color palette
- playtesting helped
- good player controls
- happy with the story
- designed on paper first
- cross platform
- deadline increased productivity
- scoreboard / highscores
- time management techniques (pomodoro etc)
- good menus / gui
- good work environment (tunes, desk, temp)
- using version control (git / svn) helped
- happy with game balance / difficulty

In terms of what typically went right, by far the most common statement was that prior knowledge and experience of your tools is of paramount importance. People really enjoyed working within the confines of a theme, and those that cut features and kept their plan simple enjoyed a stress-free Jam as a result. Jammers who had an easy way to create game levels reported benefiting from this often, and those who took the trouble to include sounds and music in their game reported being very satisfied by the decision.

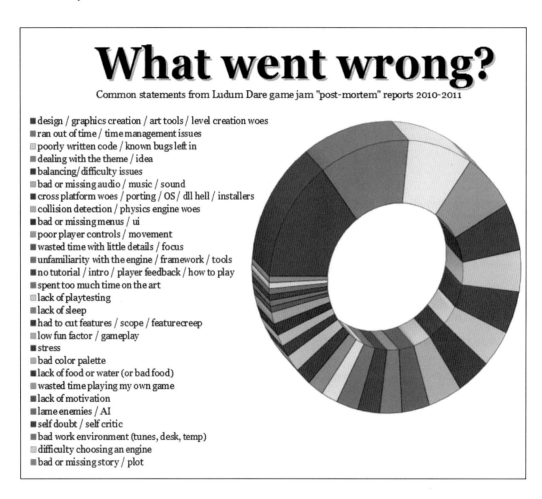

What went wrong?

Common statements from Ludum Dare game jam "post-mortem" reports 2010-2011

- design / graphics creation / art tools / level creation woes
- ran out of time / time management issues
- poorly written code / known bugs left in
- dealing with the theme / idea
- balancing/ difficulty issues
- bad or missing audio / music / sound
- cross platform woes / porting / OS / dll hell / installers
- collision detection / physics engine woes
- bad or missing menus / ui
- poor player controls / movement
- wasted time with little details / focus
- unfamiliarity with the engine / framework / tools
- no tutorial / intro / player feedback / how to play
- spent too much time on the art
- lack of playtesting
- lack of sleep
- had to cut features / scope / feature creep
- low fun factor / gameplay
- stress
- bad color palette
- lack of food or water (or bad food)
- wasted time playing my own game
- lack of motivation
- lame enemies / AI
- self doubt / self critic
- bad work environment (tunes, desk, temp)
- difficulty choosing an engine
- bad or missing story / plot

With regard to the things that typically went wrong during a Game Jam, by far the most common problem people experienced was difficulty in creating the art for their game. Not having a level editor or having to deal with a technically challenging art production pipeline will greatly affect your experience. It is quite interesting to note that it was not code bugs that troubled most Jammers: it was the creation of art and levels.

The obvious challenge of time constraints comes a natural second place, while those that struggled to find inspiration in the theme suffered as a result. Many games were created without any play-testing and as a result were unbalanced: they were generally either too easy (or more often, too hard) to play.

Surprisingly, although many Jam games do not include sound, which is a feature often left until the last minute (or the first to be dropped entirely), people who created a game devoid of sound effects or music felt that their games were significantly worse off because of it.

Overall, the primary message conveyed by these results is — Get to know your tools before the Jam. Make sure that you can create the art as easily as you can the code — especially the sound. Get people other than yourself to play-test it so it isn't too hard, doesn't have lousy controls and lame enemies, and is easy to figure out what to do. Don't bother with physics unless absolutely necessary. Prepare to deal with time-management issues, cut features and focus on what's most important. Keep your plan simple.

Don't forget the sound!

Sound is often overlooked in games, but the stats from both the "what went right" and "what went wrong" data suggest that sound and music are an integral component and greatly affect the perception of quality.

It makes sense. Ambient background noise in a game can really set the mood, and cool sound effects add so much excitement and punch to the action that it could rightly be said that a game without sound is half of a game.

Everyone knows that there isn't any sound in space...but a shooter without explosive sound effects simply doesn't feel exciting. An ominous mechanical hum in a corridor can add tension, and drips of water or wind can make a cavern beg to be explored.

A great technique used by veteran Jammers is to prepare a library of samples ready for use during the Jam. There are thousands of public domain game sounds available on the web, at sites such as `http://www.freesound.org` which can be used in your games. Tools that generate sounds specifically for games are also handy, such as `http://www.drpetter.se/project_sfxr.html` which is designed to create "retro" 8-bit sounds inspired by the likes of Super Mario Brothers.

Finally, great sound effects can be made without expensive equipment: using your own voice or blowing into a microphone and slowing it down in a sound editing program can result in some amazing effects. If you can't find the perfect sound effect, "sing it!"

Dealing with the Game Jam "theme"

Virtually every Jam requires that you try to make a game that fits a theme. This is either a surprise word that the moderators came up with or one that has been voted upon earlier.

The theme for a Jam is typically announced immediately before it begins. The anticipation and surprise gives the start of the event extra excitement and serves as a means to inspire the participants in the same way that the "secret ingredient" is used in the TV show *Iron Chef*.

Once the theme word or words have been announced, digest it for a while. Some suggestions for coming up with a great game concepts based on the theme are as follows:

- Take a walk
- Listen to music
- Mull over ideas away from the computer
- Come back home and sketch your idea
- Visualize the game being played before touching the keyboard
- Talk about the theme over dinner with a friend
- Sleep on it and start in the morning

Use this theme word as the genesis for your creative spark. Let it inspire you to think outside your normal comfort zone. Don't get discouraged if you think the theme isn't something you like: any game concept can be easily manipulated to fit a theme. Add one subtle reference and whatever game you'd hoped to make is still a possibility.

Haiku Time:
Many ideas.
They all seem to fit the theme!
Must I choose just one?

Games that tend to win Game Jam competitions often make use of the theme word to find endless material for humor.

One very strange statistical anomaly is that in most Game Jams, these three themes always score well in the voting stages: **evolution, kittens,** and **fishing**. Time and time again they are "always a bridesmaid, never a bride" and tend to be in the top ten, rather than the chosen theme. In Ludum Dare, for example, the "evolution" theme has been in the top ten almost a dozen times over the last six or seven years. When will "the evolution of kitten fishing" finally be the theme of a Game Jam?

What the experts say: *Chevy Ray Johnston*

A great way to come up with an idea to fit the theme is to write down the first five things that come to mind, then toss 'em. Those are the ideas everybody else is already thinking of and/or making.

If I could give one piece of advice to newcomers, it would be to make a really simple game, and spend all your time polishing it like crazy! Really polished games are addictive, impressive, and always popular.

Visual polish of some sort always seems to give games a boost-up in votes in compos, and makes them more likely to be clicked on by judges (especially in short Jams, where 90% of the games have little to no graphics). But unless you just care about winning, don't sacrifice a fun or engaging and interesting game just to make it look pretty.

The best thing about Game Jams is the ridiculous shortcuts and solutions developers come up with to solve design problems in such a short time span.

I hope that in the future, Game Jams will see more people developing not just video games, but other types of games as well; and creative things in general. I'm talking about writing Jams, board Game Jams, card Game Jams, and tech Jams where people get together and try to solve technological problems with the same mindset and ambition. Jams are great.

 **Chevy Ray Johnston** is author of many games including Fat Wizard and Skullpogo, the creator of the FlashPunk game engine (which is frequently used in Game Jams), and two time winner of Ludum Dare with the games FleeBuster and Beacon.

Blog: http://chevyray.com/
Twitter: http://twitter.com/chevyray
Flashpunk: http://flashpunk.net/
Google+: https://plus.google.com/103872388664329802170

An example of a winning entry

Let's take an example theme and see what it might inspire you to create. Take "ESCAPE," the theme of Ludum Dare 21.

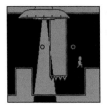

The winner of Ludum Dare 21 (theme: ESCAPE) created a game where you had to run away from an alien death beam in various platform-style obstacle courses.

Try it out: *Flee Buster* by **Chevy Ray Johnston**.
`http://chevyray.com/art/ld21/5/FleeBuster_512.swf`

Other notable entrants created puzzle games where you had to escape from a mansion, jail, dungeon, or reverse pinball where you were the ball trying to get past the bottom. The possibilities are endless.

The key qualities that the top ten entries all had were:

- Humor
- Simple gameplay
- Simple graphics
- Easy to pick up and play (simple controls)

Coming up with a plan

Once you've been given the theme, you have your team (if any), your tools are at the ready and your game engine is ready to be put to use, the next step can be the hardest: starting. Coming up with a plan takes time, and that's the one commodity in short supply during a 48 hour Game Jam.

Don't waste too many hours brainstorming, drawing flowcharts or writing a proper design document. That said, it would be foolish to forge ahead without some sort of direction. Therefore, a powerful and often used approach is to create a "minimal" design specification. Not a true design document "bible" like an AAA game team would produce, but instead a one-pager.

Building a game by first creating concept art

One way to approach your design is to create a "fake" screenshot of what you would like the game to look like in an art program (or simple drawn by hand on paper). This technique works really well, since a picture is worth a thousand words.

- Imagine your game
- Draw it in Photoshop (or scan a paper sketch)
- Chop up the image to create sprites
- Use them in your program

If you can quickly sketch a fake thumbnail of your game in action, you are able to visualize your final product. In five or ten minutes, you should be able to sketch a dozen thumbnails of game concepts this way and choose the best from the bunch.

Using graph paper or board game pieces

Another commonly used design technique for time-limited endeavors is to build a prototype of your game on paper using board game pieces. Games such as strategy and puzzle games, or rogue-like dungeon crawlers and tactics titles work best with this method.

Using plastic game pieces and graph paper (or lines drawn on a piece of paper) you might come up with a play-by-play for your game, a simple rule set, or a concept of what your first map should look like.

"First, I'm going to work on tons of amazing, detailed and polished art. Once all that is made, I'll spend the rest of the time with the code."

"I might run out of time, so I plan to first code the entire game using no art at all: just colored rectangles and circles. Once the gameplay feels fun, with the time I have left I'll replace the art with nicer looking sprites. That way for sure I'll finish before the deadline."

Don't worry about making it beautiful!

One of the key factors common to all Game Jam winners is that the games themselves aren't particularly beautiful. At the heart of gameplay is the "feel" and players will forgive simplistic, blocky stick figures if the game feels fun. Don't waste too much time sketching or creating fake screenshots that are works of art.

Concentrate on the important parts of your game
Movement
Controls
A way to "die"
Triggering a "win" state
The "feel"

Less important aspects worth saving for later include sounds and graphics, large levels, high score databases, and anything else that might be considered nonessential to the base gameplay.

Once your game functions, once you can jump around, shoot or make plot decisions, once you have created the most basic of prototypes where there is some movement or animation - only then is it worthwhile making the game world big or beautiful.

Your gorgeously hand-painted backdrop that is a masterpiece of art but isn't fun to play (or isn't finished!) will not be popular, regardless of how lovely it looks.

Avoid the latest fad—go low-tech

You can win a Game Jam with pixelated retro graphics that only use four colors. The proof of this fact is perfectly illustrated by the winning game pictured above. Many better looking games placed significantly lower in the rankings for a reason: the "feel".

By the same token, you don't have to use the latest-and-greatest technology. You can make a game in 2D instead of 3D, without any physics or amazing real-time lighting shaders. In fact, some people make games as simple web pages or games that don't even require a computer (like board games and role playing games).

Hexagon Empire—a board game designed during a Game Jam

The **Global Game Jam (GGJ)**, for example, encourages participants to look beyond videogames to any kind of game design. Board games, card games and pen-and-paper role playing games in the vein of Dungeons and Dragons have been created at this game Jam.

What the experts say: *Dr. Mike Reddy*

Did you know that even FPS game designs have been tested using paper-based prototypes? Almost all the iconic video games of the last 40 years were designed on paper first. Brenda Brathwaite, a world-renowned game designer, has even pushed the boundaries of games as art with board games such as *Train*. All the cool game designers are doing it. All it takes is paper, glue, scissors, and some pens.

What's cool about board games for the GGJ? Well, first off any bugs are people bugs. You can talk through the error, and that itself can solve the problem. Making games by playing them. No waiting to compile! No crashes or backups. No programming gurus necessary. Any room with tables and chairs will do. Bring along as many games as you are able to, it can provide something to spark off ideas, or at least something to do in the breaks. A first draft prototype can be ready to test in 15 minutes. The computer people will have only just booted their PCs by then.

Dr. Mike Reddy is Programme Leader for Games and Future Technology at the University of Wales, Newport, is a contributor to #AltDevBlogADay and helps run the Global Game Jam.

AltDevBlogADay: http://altdevblogaday.com/
GGJ Website: http://gamesoc.newport.ac.uk/GGJ/
Google+: https://plus.google.com/104325194614923361128

3
Hours 13-24:
Deeper into the Jungle!

"Try to avoid planning as much as possible, it eats time and blinds you from serendipitous opportunities."

- LiquidAsh

Stay motivated!
Keep it simple. Don't give up. Don't do too many things at the same time: lay down one feature at a time and concentrate on what is most important.

The Global Game Jam in Vancouver, Canada

In this chapter, we are going to focus on the techniques required to really dive in and plow forward toward the finish line. In particular, topics we will cover include:

- Staying motivated
- Prototyping with placeholder art
- Finding the essential mechanics
- Finishing a playable prototype early

Motivation techniques

Staying positive can be hard as the hours fly by. It is a common feeling by the end of the first day to be overwhelmed at one's lack of progress. Like in any software project, getting to the finish line always takes twice as long as you would estimate at the beginning. There are always unforeseen hassles, technical hiccups, and features that are required that you'd forgotten about.

We'll get over these by:

- Busting through "the wall"
- Showing off your progress
- Seeking support: have a chat

Getting over "The Wall"

Not giving up is the key to success. Just as a professional marathon runner knows about "the wall" (that point where you feel like giving up, like you couldn't possibly get to the finish line), if you plow past your self-doubt and smash through that wall of uncertainty you will find that at the end of the tunnel is a light. As you approach the finish line you will again become increasingly sure of yourself and your speed will increase. Soon you'll be able to taste it, it is so close.

All you have to do is get past the wall. One way to force yourself not to give up when you're feeling down and out is to take a break. Get some fresh air and approach the problem from a different angle after getting your mind off things for a while.

Share your work-in-progress

Another great motivational tool is posting screenshots of the work in progress. Sharing your work with others (your fellow Jammers, Twitter, your blog, and so on) will generate feedback and encouragement. Hearing what others think of what you've done so far can give you the little push to keep you going.

Keep in touch

Talking about your work will also give you good reason to finish, since you've publicly committed to it. It is easy to give up when you won't lose face, so post about your game everywhere so that people know what you're up to. You wouldn't want to disappoint your "fans", would you? Most importantly, engaging your peers is the best way to get a little pat on the back at just the right time. When you need it most, a simple kudos, a +1 or a like on your blog post can be all you need to renew your efforts.

Don't code in a vacuum—get out there and feel the support of others. Don't be afraid to ask for help. Get feedback from people. Show off your hard work. Encourage others and test their games, too. You'll find that whatever you give is what you'll get. If you encourage your fellow competitors, they'll do the same for you.

What the experts say: *Austin Breed*

To finish your game before the deadline, start on the hour the theme is announced, even if you only have time to jot down ideas. When you go to bed you will have the theme fresh in your mind, and sometimes the best ideas are discovered when you're in a relaxed half-sleepy state. Being able to wake up already knowing what the game will be gives you a head start; just don't forget to write it down!

A great way to come up with an idea to fit the theme is to get away from your computer and live in real life for a bit. I read somewhere that Shigeru Miyamoto created the mushroom kingdom after a walk in the woods. In my personal opinion, the best games reflect on things we feel and interact with in nature. Perhaps if more people thought like this we'd have less Call of Duties and more Katamari Damacies.

Austin Breed is one of the organizers of the Newgrounds Game Jams, a freelance artist and the creator of games such as *Covetous*, *A Mother in Festerwood*, and *Distance*.

Profile: http://austinbreed.newgrounds.com/
Game Jam: http://www.newgrounds.com/collection/nggamejams
Twitter: http://twitter.com/#!/austinbreed

4
Hours 25-36:
Breaking Through The Wall!

"What is the best way to make it to the finish line? Start smaller than you think you should, and expand as time permits."

- LiquidAsh

See that light at the end of the tunnel? It's not a train.
Don't get discouraged by slow progress. Work around the bugs. Keep your morale high and don't forget to sleep.

The Manilla Game Jam

In this chapter we will be exploring the most difficult stage of any Game Jam: the third quarter. This is the stage that many participants quit because the finish line is still far away. The easy and exciting beginning is well over and the nose-to-the-grindstone "hard part" is in full swing. Specifically, we'll explore:

- Motivation and morale
- Time management
- Simplification
- Breaking the rules
- Automation of art assets
- Iterative development

Keep It Simple, Stupid!

More important than any design document, more important than your programming skills or the fantastic game engine you have is management of your expectations. The masterwork you may wish you could make in a weekend is probably not the game that you will make in reality. One important tactic for Game Jam success is to tone down your plans. Lower your expectations. Follow the K.I.S.S. Rule – keep it simple, stupid!

The KISS rule, great as it is, is overly general. What you really need are some concrete and specific examples.

- Simplistic graphics that are quickly produced
- Simple controls (as few as possible: four or less buttons)
- Minimal game mechanics (one or two rules)
- Do one thing well, not twenty things poorly
- Make the executable "just work" without complex installation
- Avoid long intros, cinematic effects, or setup screens
- Don't craft perfect OOP code for future use: quick n dirty is fine
- Aim for less than you think you can accomplish
- Plan to finish early (everything takes longer than expected)
- Low tech is better, high tech (cutting edge) is problematic
- 2D games take a quarter of the time to code than an equivalent 3D game
- 2D art takes 1/10th the hours of designing as compared to 3D art
- When in doubt: no physics engine
- When in doubt: Square grid (as opposed to hexagons)

Since everything takes more work than expected, aim to create a game that feels "too simple". One that you initially think you could easily create in a single afternoon. You'll soon discover that even the simplest game will take many times more work than you planned. All the polish, dealing with unforeseen hassles, installation woes, learning curves and submission time will eat up your hours.

Remember that it is far better to design a simple game that is funny or witty or action packed than it is to craft a deep, rich, complex one. Also remember that most players will only play your game for one or two minutes. If they can't see nearly everything your game has to offer in the first 30 seconds, most will give up and try another game.

If you waste time with long intros, complex setup screens, laborious cinematics or tedious tutorials, the majority of users will shut down your game long before they see "the best parts" - so be sure that the best part of your game is the first ten seconds!

No-art (rectangles) gameplay proof-of-concept

Experienced game developers will often tell you that they first make the entire game with placeholder art. Instead of getting caught up in creating beautiful artwork that is polished and time consuming, program your entire game using simple geometric shapes. If your gameplay "feels right" and is fun when there is nothing more than colored rectangles or circles on screen, you have a winner.

This technique is also the key to finishing before the deadline. If you focus solely upon the art at the onset, you will likely find yourself with a good looking but broken game when the time is up. It is better to have good gameplay—make everything work first, and then make it pretty.

Once your game is fun to play, any time that remains can be confidently spent on making the art as great as the game mechanics themselves. No matter what you do, if your game works before the deadline and pressure is off—you can craft fantastic art with the confidence that your game is functional and you'll finish in time.

Distil to the essential features

Game Jams are the wrong place to aim for complex gameplay. Even when you think you've kept things simple, by the halfway mark you will probably need to trim the fat; throw out less important features, lose that second boss battle, reduce the number of levels, and simplify your game mechanics. It is better to do one thing well than try to do a dozen things that all turn out half-baked.

An incredibly fun single-level game can win a competition, but a lousy twenty-level epic will not. If your single level or single gameplay mechanic is so great that people love your game and are clamoring for more, you will have succeeded in your goal of making a fun game. You can always add more levels, more bosses, more polish at a later date.

Find the "fun" early, and distil your concept to find the most essential features. Throw out the rest.

Finishing a "working" basic prototype early

One weekend is not a lot of time. At the end of your project there are going to be unexpected problems. They might involve the creation of a downloadable package, ZIP file, or installer. Perhaps the game that works perfectly on your computer happens to need a `.dll` that others do not have. If you aim to finish your game at the very last minute, you are likely to get burned.

Instead, aim to finish several hours (or even an entire day) ahead of the deadline. Post an initial test version. Drop into one of the IRC chat rooms or forums for the Jam you're in and ask people to test out your game. They might find that it doesn't even work and you'll be glad you aimed to finish early. Those last few hours should only be used for polish, uploading files, entering in the submissions form, taking screenshots and posting about your experiences.

Many Game Jam websites lag terribly to the point of being unusable if you try to submit your entry at exactly the moment the Jam is over, since everyone else is doing the same. Don't get burned by last-minute efforts: upload an hour early and avoid all the stress.

[
Haiku time:
Three features: a crowd.
Just a second to play off the pearlescent first.
—droqen
]

Occam's Razor

Aim for a smaller game that you might hope to make. If you have extra time at the end you can easily add more features or an extra level. If your plan leaves no "wiggle room", it is quite likely that you won't be submitting anything at all when the looming deadline finally knocks at your front door.

Additionally, the more features you add to your game, in terms of a purely quantitative decision, the less likely these features will mesh happily with one another. For every new component, class, function or variable you add to your codebase, you exponentially increase the chances of a game-breaking bug.

The reason for this effect can be illustrated by considering a physical machine. Imagine one made up of only a single gear and a piston. If they work, they work. Now add twenty more gears to the mix: a bent tooth in even a single gear is sure to cause problems with the rest of the machine. The more parts there are, the more likely something will break down. In engineering, algorithms, math, science and programming, Occam's Razor is a rule that proves itself to be true time and time again.

To avoid falling prey to over-complexity, feature creep, or too many interacting, inter-dependent parts in your game, try to follow as many of these suggestions as you can:

Fewer components mean fewer bugs

> One large class versus many small ones
>
> A small number of larger source code files instead of many, many small ones
>
> Functional programming versus object-oriented programming
>
> Standalone (compartmentalized) classes vs. many dependencies
>
> AI that uses the same functions as player control
>
> Art assets that spawn gameplay versus hardcoding behaviors or levels
>
> Single platform versus cross-platform codebases
>
> Game engines that require no third-party "plugins"
>
> Compiled games with everything in one exe versus many DLLs
>
> Art creation tool-chain with as few steps to import as possible
>
> Development environments that are all-in-one versus many tools
>
> Solo efforts versus team efforts

Break the rules of computer science!

As you can tell from the previous list above, the majority of these tips and hints fly directly in the face of conventional software development wisdom. They would give any computer science professor reason to fail you in your course work. Larger studios would shake their heads in dismay, and highbrow hipster coders would call you old-fashioned.

Rebel against conventional wisdom: most of these well-known rules (for example, object-oriented is better than functional programming) work best in large projects that have the luxury of long project lifecycles. The over-engineered codebase is the "ideal" when you can take as long as you want on something. Object-oriented design is fine, but never feels guilty for using a global variable, or a single function that is 20 lines long instead of a generic, abstract OOP class, that requires several new files and a hundred extra lines of "glue code" to work in your project.

Remember, this is a speed-programming competition. You aren't going to be marked in using all the latest and greatest design patterns. In the real world of Game Jams, as well as hardcore game engine development, it turns out that abstractions, reusable code, and highly hierarchical classes with interwoven dependencies aplenty do nothing but add complexity, introduce new bugs, increase the size of your code, require more RAM and run slower!

Allow yourself to break the rules. Be a rebel: program specifically for your particular game. Make a routine that can only be used in one way, as opposed to an abstract utility class that could be used in fifty future projects. You'll save time, your code will run faster, and your project will be half the size.

The final tip in the previous list may sound completely wrong. How could a solo effort require less programming time than a group one?

Brooks' Law

The "mythical man-month" (http://en.wikipedia.org/wiki/The_Mythical_Man-Month) is a concept that was first introduced by now-famous computer science writer **Fred Brooks**. It has been proven true time and time again to the point that it is now simply referred to as **Brooks' Law**. Briefly, it describes the fact that adding more team-members to a project does not reduce development time. In many cases, the more people working on a project, the longer it will take to finish!

This might sound counter-intuitive at first, but just as the machine with more parts has a higher likelihood of breaking down, so does the team with more members. All that enthusiasm can be infectious and certainly a good team can create amazing things, but don't be fooled into thinking that doubling the size of your team will halve the development time of your project.

Haiku Time:
Coding late at night.
Can't stop now, I'm in the zone!
I'll sleep on Monday.

"War Story": Diary of a failed Game Jam

"We were sure we'd win the competition. We had the best game engine. Our coders were industry professionals. Our artist was a master. We forgot that the real battle was going to be with that most unforgiving of mistresses: Time!"

Nearly every first timer reports similar experiences after participating in a Jam for the first time: they never finished. More important than programming skill, more significant than what tools you have at the ready; it is your prowess at time management that will be the strongest influence on your success. Knowing this in advance means that the true Game Jam hero plans to do very little.

Common mistakes

After most Game Jams, dozens of users will lament how they got "burned out" or the energy fizzed out before the end of the competition.

> **Many participants quit after the first day for various reasons**
> Over-ambition
> Not accounting for unforeseen bugs
> The game wasn't fun
> Exhaustion
> The Jam itself wasn't fun (more work than expected)

The cures for these ills are: **treat yourself well**; take breaks, eat well, get a proper night's sleep. Your brain will turn to mush if you try to go full bore the entire time. This is supposed to be fun - don't forget to drink, sleep, and do other things.

Reducing production time

Your game should, by now, be playable. Perhaps there is only a single, empty room to run around in. Maybe you've got a title screen and some movement code but there's nothing much to see or do.

Consider yourself in great stead if you've reached that point. The next step is to flesh out your game world—to add enemies or puzzles or levels, or to create "gameplay" that your basic engine is capable of supporting.

Hand-crafted versus computer-generated content

Up to this point you may have, for example, decided to create a platformer game such as Super Mario Brothers. If you were smart, all you worked on was running, jumping, and collision detection so you won't fall through the ground and can't run through walls.

The next step is to create a bunch of levels that are fun to explore. There are two approaches to doing so: hand-craft your levels (which will necessarily be few in number) or let your computer help you create more content.

To create levels for your game, you may might be tempted to construct vast worlds filled with custom placed entities. If you have time, go for it - but in reality you will probably only have time to make one or two small rooms to explore. As long as it is fun, there's nothing wrong with having a very short game. If players complain that they wished there was more to play, then you know you're on to something great.

That said, if you would like larger worlds but don't have time to craft them meticulously, you can take advantage of procedurally generated content.

The most common way to create game level content uses **fractals**. For example, the built-in "Perlin noise" functions in Flash are often used to generate outdoor geographical features like mountains and lakes. Pure random numbers that are constrained to follow a few rules can produce very realistic dungeons, cities and forest, given a few simple formulae. For example, generate random noise and then "blur" the result, smoothing out the values to average out those of their neighbors to make the changes gradual.

Maze generation and terrain algorithms are easy to find using Google. Why not take advantage of them and set up a few simple rules that can generate infinite levels?

Iterating the prototype to find the fun

Many times people exclaim after a Game Jam that they'd set off in one direction, but halfway through, a bug or glitch in the game prototype was so fun to fiddle around with that they made the decision to incorporate this accidental feature into the primary game mechanic. If you find something fun - no matter how unplanned, pump it up and go with it!

If your game works but seems lackluster, then you will need to tweak it a little to "find the fun". This can be as simple as changing the amount of gravity in your world (suddenly your boring platformer becomes a frantic moon adventure) or the speed of your movement (zipping around in the world as opposed to a dull crawl). Occasionally all it takes is a little more bombast: add more enemies or some funny sounds.

Example of a winning entry

The winner of Ludum Dare 20 (theme: It's Dangerous to go Alone! Take This! – `http://www.ludumdare.com/compo/ludum-dare-20/?action=top`) created a beautiful platformer with unique pixel graphics. Try it out: **Sebastien Bernard's** *Appy 100mg* – `http://dl.dropbox.com/u/4952054/ludumdare20/postRelease/index.html`

Whatever the case may be, you should stop creating brand new game features by the halfway point in the Jam and try to focus upon the feel; the soul or fun factor. Elusive as it may be, all it takes is a little play-testing and tweaking to turn a game from a passable but forgettable one to something everyone is talking about. It might be the simple addition of some humor.

Perhaps your platformer is great as-is, in terms of feel, but would be more memorable if, instead of a plumber walking around on bricks the player was a microscopic adventurer stuck inside someone's head bouncing around on globs of brain matter. The coding remains the same but a quick change to the art and sounds and suddenly you have something more silly, fresh, and original.

FIRST make it work, THEN make it pretty

Remember that many of the more popular winning entries from previous Game Jams do not have beautiful graphics. All that really matters to players is the feel. If your game crashes or has any game-stopping bugs, nobody will like it no matter how beautiful the title screen.

If your game works great on level one but crashes on level two, either find and fix the bug (if you can do so in time) or simply eliminate level two entirely! Less is more: one level that functions is better than two that crash.

Because time is the most precious commodity at this point, you can safely assume that you will not be able to eliminate every bug.

The best techniques at this point are

Comment out buggy code instead of fixing it

Remove gameplay mechanics that cause problems

Improve the features that work instead

Don't fixate on the bug or get stuck

Ignore the problem if it is minor: imperfection is okay

Don't let a bug be a roadblock: move on

What the experts say: *Christopher Nilssen*

Make it playable above all else. Worry the most about whether the player can get into the game, perform the actions you want them to, and then get out again gracefully. And even that last part can be ignored in favor of having a couple of working features.

Forget art, forget sound, forget animated UIs and particles and all the other bells and whistles until you have a playable that you're having fun with.

Other Jammers and judges will get it, they know the conditions of the event and will be happy to run through an abstraction of what your game is, rather than needing fully modeled and textured characters with voice acting.

Christopher "Jack" Nilssen is an independent game developer, fiction writer, runner, yogi, and lover who is awake before you in the morning. He runs Dark Acre Game Development, a studio committed to producing a game experience every two months in order to generate market awareness and gain a deeper appreciation for all aspects of the game development processes, both commercial and artistic. He is the author of three books and developer of games such as The Child, Ball of Steel, and Above and Below.

Website: http://dark-acre.com/

Twitter: http://Twitter.com/#!/DarkAcreJack

5

Hours 37-48:
Getting to the Finish Line!

Here comes the fun part!
Embrace your inner hacker. Cut out any weak parts. Drop features.
Work on gameplay and polish. Do one thing well and trim the fat.

The Amaze Festival Game Jam

In this chapter we will explore the final stage of a Game Jam: the most exciting part.
Not only can you see the light at the end of the tunnel but your game is most likely
almost done. You may be completely exhausted, but by breaking through the wall
and making it to the end you will feel a new surge of energy as the finish line draws
nearer. Scrambling to submit your game on time, you will start to work faster and
faster, frantically racing toward the final product. Topics we will cover include:

- How to finish your game on time
- Avoiding headaches and hassles

- What to do when in danger of missing the deadline
- Allowing for imperfection
- Cutting features and ignoring bugs
- Common features of winning games
- Adding polish and testing the game
- Packaging and submitting your game
- The importance of the name, description and icon

"Captain's log"—diary of a winning entry

"We had all these grandiose plans. We initially had a twenty page design document, filled with sketches. We thought this would save us some time. Instead of finishing the game as designed, the only way we were able to pull anything off within the time limit at all was to throw out 90% of what we'd planned and focus on the one mechanic that we'd gotten to work. All that work we did in the middle of the project was buggy and broken and we didn't have time to fix it."

"Instead of giving up and simply not submitting anything, we realized that the basic 'shooter' mechanic that we'd implemented in the first couple hours of the Game Jam were enough to feel 'fun' all on their own. We pared down the game to its most basic essence."

"We threw virtually everything out: all the boss battles, all the puzzle elements, and what we had left was a simple, fun area shooter. Nothing more. The amazing thing is that in so doing, we had extra time on our hands to polish this one mechanic and really make it fun. We had time to tweak the movement speeds and firing rates and made the game so much better by doing one thing and doing it well. Everything else that we'd planned was just noise. It was just fat that had to be trimmed."

Avoiding headaches

Real life counts, too. If the Jam is getting you down, or if you have barely slept at all during the entire weekend, you are at risk of severe burnout. Remember that there is a real live world filled with people who care about you out there, and they'll keep on caring whether or not your game is a masterpiece or not.

When you find that your morale is really low, or if you have a pounding headache, aching muscles or are so tired that your productivity has slowed to a standstill, go outside. Take a break.

If your partner is so annoyed at the long hours you've spent away from them, ask yourself which is more important? Spending some time with the person you love or making your game? The answer should be clear. Jams are fun, and it can be sad to participate in one and not finish, but real life is far more important.

Treat yourself well, and listen for the warning signs. At least half of your fellow competitors will drop out of the race before reaching the finish line: there's no shame in trying and not finishing. Even setting out to make a game and not finishing it by the deadline is a fun experience: you'll have learned a lot, set up your tools more efficiently, and gained some valuable practice that will help you the next time you're up to bat.

What the experts say: *Pekka Kujansuu*

The worst way to prepare for a Game Jam is to stay up all night so you can be there for the theme announcement if it's at night. Before you start programming, if possible, take a walk or a shower to get some thinking or brainstorming done without staring at a screen. Come up with a few different ideas to pick from, and remember to ask and answer the question: What does the player *do* in the game?

To finish your game before the deadline, don't get caught up on polishing or deciding whether the player character has green or blue hair. Toss out unnecessary extra features unless you have a lot of time left after finishing the core game.

A great way to come up with an idea to fit the theme is to look up the dictionary definition of the theme. Google an image on the theme. Check what the Wikipedia page for the theme says.

If I could give one piece of advice to newcomers, it would be: *Don't worry about your game being shit*. It probably will be, and that's all right! Your next game will be better!

Pekka "pekuja" Kujansuu is a Ludum Dare administrator, creator of Screenshotsaturday and author of games such as *Tiny Hawk*, which is available on the web (Flash) and on the PSP Minis platform (and Playstation network).

Website: http://polygontoys.com/
Screenshotsaturday: http://screenshotsaturday.com/
Twitter: http://Twitter.com/pekuja
Google+: https://plus.google.com/108792302762385685386

What to do when you think you might not finish

As the final twelve hours tick down you might be able to see that at the rate you're going, there is simply no possible way you can finish. This is the perfect time to change direction. For example, throw out half your game design. Make a joke game that is impossible to win.

Ways to finish when all seems lost

Buggy? Find something fun about it and call it a feature!

Only one level? Call it a "battle arena!"

Broken weapons? Make the game an "avoider" with no guns!

Sound broken? Your main character is deaf—or in space!

Not fun yet? Make it a "joke game" meant to annoy players!

Ugly art? Call it retro, hipster, or ironic!

Poor framerate? Make it a turn-based strategy!

No story or characters? This is an arcade title!

No gameplay or all story? This is a visual novel!

No "game over" or way to die? Can you survive for 60 seconds?

Code won't compile? Comment out parts until it does!

Too tired to finish? Call it done right now and submit!

It works but it sucks? Take pride in the fact that you finished!

I could do so much better! Next time you will!

Don't beat yourself up!

Don't let your pride stop you from submitting whatever you were able to accomplish. After spending an entire weekend working on your game, you are sure to be your harshest critic. What you may think of as a buggy mess without any redeeming features, others with fresh eyes may call a game with "tons of potential!" More importantly, it is better to finish something that people can play than it is to aim for perfection and never finish at all. Give yourself a break and remember that the goal here is to have a little fun.

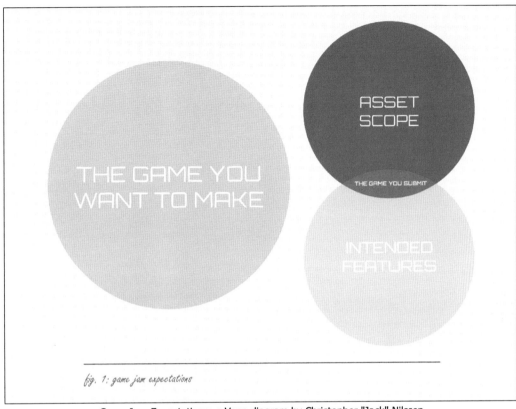

fig. 1: game jam expectations

Game Jam Expectations: a Venn diagram by Christopher "Jack" Nilssen

Much like a jazz improvisation Jam, a Game Jam has to allow for mistakes. Like the master jazz guitarist who attempts a solo that doesn't quite sound perfect, it isn't how perfect your performance is or how few the mistakes you make; it is the "soul" of your artistic endeavor that counts. Even with mistakes, a guitar solo played with conviction and energy will still be loved by your audience. Just as a vocal performance sung with conviction and emotion is far more respected that one sung with robotic perfection but no style. People will forgive the imperfections when your game is viewed as a whole.

Cut-and-run: chop out the bad parts

Do one thing, and do it well. Complex, buggy systems are worse than simple, polished ones. In design and art, a common phrase attributed to **Antoine de Saint-Exupéry** perfectly sums this up: *"Perfection is achieved, not when there is nothing left to add, but when there is nothing left to remove"*.

The best designs are the simplest. When in doubt, leave it on the cutting room floor. As has been mentioned above, with regard to bugs and simply commenting out parts that don't work, your game might also benefit from the removal of anything mediocre. Instead of a vast landscape devoid of fun, a single tiny room filled with gameplay will wow audiences far more often.

If you can, try to concentrate the fun-factor. Condense your game world. Do more with less. If your cinematic intro drags on too long, trim some of the fluff, or simply speed up the character's speech in a sound editing program so that they talk faster.

Instead of long introduction screens filled with text that nobody will read, throw players into the action from the get-go. The vast majority of players trying out your game will immediately skip any blocks of text longer than two sentences. Assume that nobody will read your wonderfully-written plot outline and most will get annoyed if they have to click more than twice before getting to the action.

Heinous hacks and ugly code are A-OK.

You're not here to get an A+ in a university computer science class, nor are you going to show this source code to prospective employers. This is a speed-coding competition. Shortcuts aren't just allowed, they are encouraged.

Hack away—you're not here for style points

OOP is highly overrated: Break the rules!

Functional or data-oriented programming is faster to write.

Copy-and-paste is allowed: Whatever saves time!

Don't program for "generic" game constructs.

Don't code with reusability in mind: One-offs are best.

Example of a winning entry

The winner of Ludum Dare 19 (Theme: Discovery | http://www.ludumdare.com/ compo/ludum-dare-19/?action=top) created a time travelling puzzle platformer. Try it out: *Time Pygmy* (http://bit.ly/ AkYFGk) by **Sebastien Bernard**.

Common features of winning Game Jam games

Now that we've been introduced to some of the top-rated Game Jam games from the last few years, it is interesting to note some of the many commonalities. Firstly, almost every single game that won was a platformer. It seems that people do not look as highly upon shooters or highly experimental titles. It makes sense: people are comfortable running and jumping. They like to explore.

There is room for creative freedom in terms of the graphics, but players can enjoy the instant gratification of already knowing how to control the game. From its origins in Super Mario Brothers and beyond, platformers have always been very popular. They sell well, even in the AAA games industry, yet are simple enough to be created in 48 short hours.

Naturally, not all winning games are of the platformer genre. It could be argued, however, that there is a statistically significant proportion of winning games of this type.

Therefore, if you want the best possible chance to rank highly in a Game Jam that has a judging component, create a beautiful, colorful, easy-to-control puzzle platformer.

Another feature shared by a significant proportion of top-rated Game Jam games is blocky pixel art. One possible reason for this is that compared to detailed 3D art, which requires a master artist and hundreds of hours of labor, a simple 16x16 sprite can convey the general idea and be made in a minimal amount of time.

More importantly, bad 3D art is simply ugly. Pixel art on the other hand allows players to "fill in the details" using their own imaginations. When you only have four pixels for an entire face, dots for eyes is fine. If you are rendering a complex 3D scene, you'll need eyelashes, eyebrows, whites, and an iris to avoid looking incorrect. Better to let one's imagination fill in the details.

Finally, pixel art is popular with players because it harkens back to "old school" days of arcade games and 8-bit consoles. The happy memories that players have of Super Mario Brothers, Gauntlet, or Pac-Man are transferred to any game with similar blocky graphics. Conversely, any photorealistic 3D art needs to be on a par with recent masterworks on next-gen consoles, and is therefore compared to games such as Skyrim, Mass Effect, Halo, and the Call of Duty series.

Which style of art do you think you can most successfully compete with?

Polish, polish, polish

It is unwise to keep working on your game until the very last minute. It would be far better to finish with many hours to spare. Not only will your stress levels be lower, but it lets you move on to the final and equally important phase of any software development project: beta testing, packaging and submitting!

Beta testing: fixing the difficulty and controls

If you get a chance to ask your fellow competitors, friends and family to play-test your game, you will likely find major problem areas worthy of extra attention. Often the game you've been working on seems easy to you (because you're intimately familiar with it). Hand it to someone who has never tried it out and watch as they struggle with the difficulty.

It is a common occurrence that the game developer assumes everyone will know exactly what to do when faced with their game for the first time. It all seems so obvious to you. The truth of the matter is that testers will probably not figure out what they're supposed to be doing, or won't be able to work the controls, or will wander aimlessly, not knowing that "there was a door just to the right of the first screen".

Letting players try out your game without giving them any verbal instructions can be a great technique to see if the game is as self-explanatory as you may think it is. You will often be surprised by how inept a first-time player is and you should adjust the difficulty accordingly.

In particular, key combinations or control mechanisms that are complex turn off players—especially those who are only going to give your game the 60-second demo. After a Game Jam, many players quickly try out every game they can—often for only mere seconds. If you can't "hook" them in the first 15 seconds, you've lost a player.

To make your game more fun for new players
Use simple controls (one button, and so on).
Throw your best content at them first.
Dive into the action: No long intros.
Make it easier than you think it should be.
Tell users exactly what to do: Don't make then guess.
Don't overload their senses: Simplify the GUI.

Packaging your game

Just because you have completed programming your game doesn't mean your work is done. You have to get it from your computer into the hands of others. This often means you will need several hours of additional time at the end of the Game Jam, so plan accordingly!

To prepare your game for distribution
Take screenshots (and videos) of the game in action.
ZIP up your game folder (or create an installer).
Upload the package to the appropriate website.
Get beta testers to download the game and try it out.
Fix any game-breaking mistakes like missing files.

Once you've prepared a "release package" for your game and confirmed that it works, you can move on to the final phase.

"I'll need all the time I can get, so I'm going to work on the game all the way to the last 30 minutes. I'm sure that's enough time to compile and package the game and upload it somewhere and fill out my entry form and take screenshots and post a blog entry..."

"I find that there are always last-minute hassles, so I'm planning to call my game finished four hours before the deadline. Once I'm done I'll ask some friends to test it all out, just in case I forgot to include a DLL or one of my URLs has a typo."

Submitting your game

Now that you've finished programming your game, and you've had some friends test it out on their computers to ensure your archive or installer works, you are ready to submit it to the Game Jam website.

This submissions process can take more time than you may expect. Planning to do this step in the final five minutes of a Jam will likely result in disaster. There's always much more to do than you expected.

Things you will need to prepare prior to submitting your game
A fantastic, short, witty name.
An engaging, brief, positive written description.
Several attractive, action-packed screenshots.
A square thumbnail or icon image.
The URL to your game's distributable.

Attractive screenshots are absolutely essential to convince people to download or play your game. Choose two or three of your best screenshots. Assembling a small collection of good ones is better than a dozen mediocre images.

Choose images with high contrast and lots of color. Big shapes are better than images with high complexity that become muddy when viewed at small sizes. Avoid screens full of text as these won't be readable when viewed as thumbnails.

People want to see the gameplay, not your title screen, so take some screenshots of the coolest-looking sections of your actual game. If you happen to catch an explosion in mid-animation or are able to highlight the piece of art that you're most proud of, all the better!

The importance of your game's name

All Game Jams list games using some sort of database query. When no query parameters are given, the default sort is nearly always alphabetical. Therefore, though it could be considered "gaming the system" a name that starts with a letter from the top of the alphabet is more likely to appear on the first page of search results. Statistics have proven that games that start with the letter A (or a number or symbol) do get a higher number of plays. That said, the practice of naming one's game solely to be on the top of the list is considered rude and cheap—so tread carefully.

More importantly than gaming the system to be listed first, the actual words you use in your game name matter a lot. Long names tend to be cut off in search results and web page titles, or word-wrap makes your game look poorly formatted. Therefore, the shorter the better. One to four words is the best target to aim for.

Titles that evoke mental imagery or describe your game in an abstract way are better than obscure or made-up words, but this rule is not universal. Many great games have completely imaginary words as the title. That said, many games names do indeed describe the action in the game in subtle ways, whether one considers Call of Duty, Boulderdash, Street Fighter, or Sim City. Even abstract names evoke emotion and imagination if they are doing their job well.

The importance of your game's description

Firstly, you need to write a short description of your game. Players will see this on your download page, and just like a search result, web page description meta tag, or online store page, this text is absolutely essential and will affect your rankings. A well-written description of your game will double the number of plays that your game gets, and pull players in with drama, a sense of adventure, conflict, or humor.

One original idea is better than a tediously long description of everything in the game. Nobody wants a screen full of text, so keep it short and simple. If your description gives players an idea of what to expect, even better. A "call to action" works well.

For example, compare these two descriptions for the same hypothetical platformer:

- "Can you jump fast enough to escape the evil death bunnies?"
- "My game was programmed in C++ and uses box2d physics and a-star pathfinding. The objective is to navigate the city in order to avoid the AI enemies."

Which would you try out first?

The importance of your thumbnail icon

Finally, most Game Jam websites and Flash game portals will represent your game with a tiny "icon" image. Often it is only the size of a postage stamp, perhaps 50x50 pixels. If you are given the option, choose a really colorful, easy-to-see image for your thumbnail, icon or primary screenshot. When faced with a page full of games, you want this one tiny image to really stand out, so use high contrast images.

Studies on user behavior have proven time and time again that it is a bad choice to simply use a screenshot of your title screen for this icon. Players will usually chose to click an icon that shows an in-game shot or an attractive character instead. If you are going to use an image with any text on it, make it easy to read even if the image is minuscule. It can be a great idea to include the title of your game in this image as long as it is easy to read, but don't forget a punchy image or character that gives players an indication of what the game is all about.

A large study was performed on a vast number of Flash games to decide which had the best and worst icons. You can learn a lot by comparing these images.

Top 100 icons (best)

http://www.flashgamelicense.com/vote_icons_results.php?top100=1

Bottom 100 icons (worst)

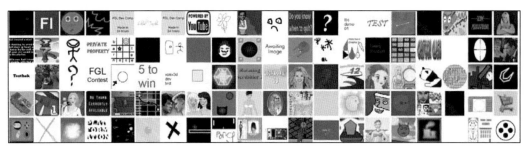

http://www.flashgamelicense.com/vote_icons_results.php?bottom100=1

What the experts say: *Foaad Khosmood*

It's not about winning. It would be a disaster if you are not having fun. If I could give one piece of advice to newcomers, it would be: Don't take it so seriously.

Before you start programming, you should ask yourself if you need to make a digital game at all.

To finish your game before the deadline, get a working version out in a few hours, then just improve it.

 **Foaad Khosmood** is an assistant professor of Computer Science at Cal Poly State University, and a director for the IGDA Global Game Jam.

Website: http://people.ucsc.edu/~foaad/

Google+: https://plus.google.com/102067858037967992680

6
After the Jam:
Fame and Fortune!

"If you don't fail the first couple of times, you're not doing it right."

- Spliter

Congratulations! You did it!

Pat yourself on the back. Get some rest. Play games made by your fellow Jammers. Put the word out. Listen to player feedback. Maybe you can polish the game and get thousands of people playing it...

The Nordic Game Jam

In this chapter, we are going to explore the next step: taking your game beyond the Game Jam. You need not stop polishing or adding to your game after the Jam ends. There's a whole world of people out there who might just want to buy it! Often the Jam version of your game serves as a mere prototype, a proof-of-concept of a particular gameplay mechanic, which if sufficiently expanded upon could be the genesis of a professional videogame worth buying. Don't stop now!

Topics that we will explore in this chapter include:

- Voting on games by your fellow developers
- Writing a post-mortem
- Preparing the game for final release
- Attracting sponsorships or advertisers
- Getting your game on app stores and portals

The voting process

Not all Game Jams include voting or rating games as part of the process. Many never declare an official "winner", but there are a few that treat the Game Jam as more of a competition, with virtual "award ceremonies" or "trophies". These kinds of Jams usually have a voting phase where participants get a chance to try out each other's games and offer feedback.

Generating goodwill among your competitors isn't just important because people that like you will vote your game more generously. It also feels good to be nice to people. When you play other people's games, you can give them a lift with positive feedback, kudos, and congratulations. Even if you found some bugs or have ideas for its improvement, be sure to point out something that you actually liked about their game first.

What the experts say: *Phil Hassey*

Game Jamming is like the most important thing ever for learning game design!

Your game has to be done a good six hours before the deadline so that you can spend a few final hours on polish and then packaging. Packaging is super important because if nobody can play your game—NOBODY WILL!!

If I could give one piece of advice to newcomers, it would be: have fun! And be sure to have all your tools ready beforehand, do a dry run of your process with a super-tiny game like Snake from start to finish. That way, your time will be spent on making a game, not getting your tools working or your packaging stuff smoothed out.

Pro strategy: Come up with a vague game idea and then go for graphics first. Sometimes getting the aesthetic down can really help you develop a unique gameplay.

Don't give up! Remember your prize is your game!

 **Phil Hassey**, manly teetotaler, creator of *Galcon*, and proud goat owner, won the IGF Innovation in Mobile Game Design award for *Galcon* in 2009. When he isn't wandering aimlessly or playing the fiddle, he'll be coding like mad and co-organizing Ludum Dare. Previously, he was webmaster for `pygame.org` and buried skeletons in a surreal mountain town. Now he drives a '59 Plymouth Fury and wants to buy a pair of giraffes.

Galcon: `http://www.galcon.com`

Blog: `http://www.philhassey.com`

Twitter: `http://Twitter.com/philhassey`

Google+: `https://plus.google.com/115283698152321681798`

The next steps: post - Jam professionalism

Once you have finished making your game, one final challenge awaits; submitting it to a website so it can be played by others. In many cases you should take several screenshots, write a brief description that "sells" your game and encourages others to play it.

Some Jams require that you also share your source code to prove it was made in a single weekend. You will likely have forms to fill out, and you might have to create a `.zip` file or even an installer for your game.

"I'm using a super-advanced engine that needs access to the registry and adds DLLs to your Windows system folder, so it requires admin permissions. Therefore I'm going to package the game in a huge installer that users will need to run so it can copy files all over their hard drive. My framework also requires users to download three other redistributables that they need to get elsewhere and install first. I'm sure it won't take more than 50 clicks and 20 minutes to get up and running, and I know everyone will say yes to all the security warnings."

"I hate installers: They require trust and can kill your computer. Also, players are lazy and want instant gratification, so I'm going to make sure that everything the game requires comes in a single .zip file that can be run anywhere without needing additional downloads or any disk access. My executable will be "polite" and will run in a security sandbox—it is portable and would work in a read-only location with no admin permissions, and it has no dependencies or weird security warnings. I might even just make a Flash, Unity, or HTML5 game so that everyone can play it in a single click without any downloads required at all. That way, everyone will play it."

You should labor to make it as easy as possible for others to play your game. Nobody wants to spend half an hour clicking and downloading and unzipping and accepting security warnings and finding missing DLLs or downloading third-party dependencies.

Try to ensure that your game is

> Either a web game (Flash, Unity, or HTML),
>
> or a standalone .zip file (no installers required)
>
> Ready to be played without any other downloads required
>
> Bug-free (get friends to test it out first)
>
> Small enough to download quickly (under 50 megs)

Writing a post-mortem analysis

The games industry website www.gamasutra.com and Game Developer Magazine popularized the game "post-mortem". This is typically a short document or blog post. They have become so important and respected in the games industry that oftentimes the post-mortem article is the lead story on the cover of the magazine.

What goes into a game post-mortem?

- An introduction (describing the game)
- What went right (victories, things that you are proud of)
- What went wrong (mistakes, disasters, problems)
- Conclusion (listing tools, team members, and stats)

The formal description of the post-mortem document as used by big-budget AAA studios in magazine articles and websites is as follows:

- A brief description of what your game was originally intended or visualized as, before the coding began.
- The type of game, the goals of the game, the intended audience.
- Specific technologies or features that you wanted to build into it that would set it apart from the competition.
- Development team and tools you used in developing the game. Five goals, features or aspects of the project went off without a hitch or better than planned. Five goals, features, or aspects of the project that were problematic or failed completely.

   Excerpted from `http://www.gdmag.com/postmort.htm`

This tradition of writing a post-mortem has now carried over into the Game Jam scene, and after any big Jam you will find a dozens of post-mortem blog posts outlining the trials and tribulations experienced by your fellow competitors. This is the perfect venue to learn from your own mistakes as well as those of others.

Many times, the same few problems crop up again and again and are repeated in the majority of post-mortems.

Most common problems reported in game post-mortems
Aiming too high: Scope issues and featurecreep
Tool limitations: Trouble importing assets and creating art
Packaging annoyances: Missing DLLs or installer woes
Running out of time or motivation

A detailed statistical analysis of big-budget AAA studio post-mortems can be found at `http://www.gamasutra.com/view/feature/6309/dissecting_the_post-mortem_lessons_.php?print=1`. Their results indicated that 71% reported scope problems where there was either not enough time or resources to complete the game, or there was too much design that had to be cut. **Featurecreep**; limiting the scope and cutting features, is by far the most common thing that you will encounter when reading game post-mortems.

You can find a massive list of Game Jam post-mortems here: `http://www.ludumdare.com/compo/tag/post-mortem/`.

There's a lot to be learned from these reports. Read em — and weep!

Finally, here is an exhaustive list of dozens of indie and AAA post-mortems that are well worth checking out: `http://www.pixelprospector.com/the-big-list-of-post-mortems/`

Sponsors, portals, and app stores

Many of the games that did well in Game Jams went on to become commercial successes. Even if you didn't win the competition, it might be wise to spend a few weeks polishing your game and releasing it on a game portal. Before you simply give it away to the public however, try attracting the interest of a sponsor.

If you made a Flash or Unity game, you can put your game up for bidding at **FGL** (`www.flashgamelicense.com`) which is a major and well respected source for Flash (and Unity) games that attract large amounts of money.

A sponsor will typically pay you a few thousand dollars to put their logo and links to their site on your game in order to attract hits to their game portal website. Many Jammers can make decent money going this route. Give it a try!

There are many places that offer game sponsorships, especially for Flash games in particular. For example, check out this encouraging Google search, which at the time of writing includes links to many game portals that are looking for games to sponsor:

`www.google.com?q=sponsorship+for+your+game`

Earning sponsorships for games is generally achieved by negotiating a price for exclusivity (your game will only appear on a particular site for a small period of time) as well as the sponsor's logo and links on your game's main menu. Many games are sponsored for a few hundred dollars but high quality (or popular) games can demand in excess of $5,000.

Aside from game portal sponsorships, there are many other opportunities out there for indie game developers to take their polished (post-Jam) games to the public. A great article that outlines other ways to monetize your game can be found here:

```
http://freetoplay.biz/2010/03/08/monetizing-your-game-outside-of-
sponsorship-flash-gaming-summit/
```

For example, multiple smaller games can be sold in collections like the **Humble Indie Bundle** (`http://www.humblebundle.com/`), and really polished games can make good money being sold on sites such as **Steam** (`http://store.steampowered.com/`), **Showmethegames** (`http://www.showmethegames.com/`), **Desura** (`http://www.desura.com/`), **Indiecity** (`http://www.indiecity.com/`) and others. There are hundreds of game publishing portals worth investigating. You can also sell your game on your own website.

You've got nothing to lose: it is entirely possible that with some time and effort a game that started out as a humble Game Jam entry could end up earning you a respectable income.

Finally, remember that the average game developer doesn't make millions of dollars. Sure, there are exceptions to the rule like millionaire Markus Persson (Notch) of Minecraft, who is a Game Jam veteran. Perhaps you too will someday be a successful as he has become. Take heart in knowing that there was a time when he was a lowly Jammer—just like you—who made games simply for the fun of it.

What the experts say: *Chris Hopp*

The best thing about Game Jams is hanging out in IRC and seeing other people's games evolve into something great (most of the time).

Before you start programming, you should probably have at least a rough plan or idea of what you want the game to be. Just programming without guidance is like doodling... Also be sure to leave some time at the end for testing, packaging and uploading.

For Ludum Dare 9, "Build the level you play", I had my honeymoon scheduled to start on the 2nd day of the competition. So, I only had 24 hours to make my game. I ended up making a somewhat complete game (it was lacking in the gameplay department, but at least it was functional). I worked on it right up until I had to leave my apartment to go catch the plane.

With this game I did the development a little backwards. After planning a little bit, I usually jump into coding, but this time I did all the graphics first, then did the coding. I may adopt this methodology for future competitions because as I'm working on the graphics, I can think of more ideas and such.

Chris "fydo" Hopp is one of the Ludum Dare administrators and would be really happy if you could vote for the "Kittens" theme.

Blog: http://fydo.net
Twitter: http://Twitter.com/fydo

You made it!

If you make it all the way to the end of a Game Jam and are lucky (and skilled) enough to finish a game, you might ask yourself, "was it all worth it?"

Even if you don't make any money from the game you made, the reward for your hard work is the game itself. It only cost you 48 short hours of your life, and forevermore you can think back to the hectic and exciting weekend that gave birth to a game of your very own that people played—and enjoyed!

Game Jamming has many additional benefits. You will learn to design intelligently and code quickly. You will learn about crunch-time and feature-creep. You will get a chance to network with hundreds of people who share the same passion for game development as you. You will get to play dozens (or even hundreds) of brand new games, made by your peers. You may even make some new friends.

Most Game Jams don't have cash prizes. No trophies. No award ceremonies. The most important prize that you can win is your game. This, in itself, is a worthy goal and something to be proud of.

If you found the inspiration and motivation to finish a Game Jam, you will have likely experienced productivity on a scale that most programmers and designers never achieve during their normal day-to-day work.

For some final wisdom on the subject of Game Jams, we will quote Foaad Khosmood, director of the Global Game Jam:

> *Game Jams are where the creative flow is devastatingly beautiful.*

This sums up the Game Jam experience perfectly. The reckless abandon, frantic pace, and creative limitations of a theme and a time-limit can give rise to works of incredible originality, free from the rules of software design; chaotic, but controlled, like riding an ocean wave; beautiful, but risky, like a jazz improvisation; exhausting, but exciting like winning a boss battle.

A worthwhile experience indeed.

A
Game Jams

Finding a Jam: a list of Game Jams around the world

Many Game Jams require that you register before the scheduled weekend. Some are held at university computer labs, others in office spaces or people's homes, and many are only done over the Internet. Events with well-stocked computer labs, prizes, and catering can cost money, so you'll need to do some research. Others still are completely free, and the only prize is the finished game you'll have at the end of it. Even these events often require pre-registration in the form of signing up on a website or blog, so you have an account with them.

Here's a list of popular Jams, but many more exist and can be found online. New Jams come into existence all the time while others may not be held next year. Search around and you are sure to find something that appeals to you.

The Global Game Jam

http://globalgamejam.org/

With tens of thousands of participants, this yearly event takes the cake for being the best organized, most popular Game Jam in the world. It is held in late January each year and there are hundreds of local events synchronized to occur on that same weekend.

Ludum Dare

http://www.ludumdare.com/compo/

With a ten year history, **Ludum Dare** (Latin for *giving game*) is the biggest and most popular non-sponsored community of Game Jammers around. Every four months over one thousand participants vote on a theme and try to write a game in a weekend. Mini Jams are held once per month, but these are more intimate affairs with around 20 participants. By comparison, the 21st Ludum Dare, which was held in August 2011, resulted in 599 games being made, and Ludum Dare 22, held in December 2011, produced a whopping 891 games. At this rate, the ten-year anniversary in April 2012 may reach the thousand games mark. Highly recommended.

The Experimental Gameplay Project

http://experimentalgameplay.com/

Once a month, these freewheeling dandies pick an interesting theme and give participants seven days worth of effort during the entire month to come up with a game based on it. Less competitive than Ludum Dare, there aren't any massive voting phases or rankings but this Game Jam is perfect for people who can't devote a single weekend to game development, and would prefer to space out the work when it better suits their schedules.

The Game Prototype Challenge

http://gameprototypechallenge.com/

Smaller and more personal, this up-and-coming Game Jam generally results in between ten and thirty games being produced, and is held over an entire week, rather than just a single weekend. Friendly and informal.

The Super Friendship Club

http://superfriendshipclub.com/

Super Friendship Club is an informal and friendly place for people to talk about games they're making and get feedback on them. They host "pageants" every two months, where participants make games around a certain theme.

Klik of the Month Klub

`http://www.glorioustrainwrecks.com/`

The folks at Glorious Trainwrecks have been hosting insanely fast two-hour Game Jams for several years now. Frenetic, fun, and fantastic.

PyWeek

`http://www.pyweek.org`

If you make games in Python, PyWeek is a popular Game Jam with theme voting, judging and some passionate fans.

Reddit Game Jams

`http://www.reddit.com/r/RedditGameJam`

Held infrequently, Game Jams at Reddit can be a great way to meet tons of your fellow game developers.

Newgrounds Game Jams

`http://www.newgrounds.com/collection/nggameJams`

There are occasional Game Jams held at all of the major Flash game portals online. These can gain you a very large audience of players quickly.

TIGJam

`http://www.tigjam.com/`

A yearly event held by the good people of TIGsource, an indie game development community.

Dream.Build.Play

`http://www.dreambuildplay.com`

A high profile one-per-year Game Jam for people who make indie games on the Xbox. Large audience, big cash prizes and a lot of really high quality games.

Blitzkast

`http://www.thepoppenkast.com/tag/blitzkast/`

A small, informal and fun Game Jam that is held almost monthly.

 There are quite literally over a hundred other Game Jams worth checking out online and new ones appear every month. Here is a listing of many Jams:

`http://www.mcfunkypants.com/2010/game-jams-aplenty/`

B
Game Engines

Choosing a game engine

You shouldn't use a Game Jam to learn a new engine. After all, writing a game engine is something that can take months or years, and if all you have is a weekend, you want to spend your time working on the actual gameplay and not fiddling with low-level initializations.

Virtually all Game Jams allow you to start with a working "base code" of routines that implement common game development tasks. You are rarely forced to truly start from scratch, so most Game Jammers use a pre-existing game engine and start from there.

If you already know how to program games, you likely already have a favorite game engine. It could be one you've made yourself, or an engine that you know and love from previous projects.

If you are just starting out and don't know any, here are some that are really easy to learn. They're all perfectly adequate to produce fun games. The choices are virtually endless and each person has a preferred engine depending on whether they are targeting the web, mobile, consoles, 3D, or 2D. Some common game creation tools that are used by thousands of Jammers include:

Flixel
Great for Flash 2D games: `http://flixel.org/`

FlashPunk
Another fantastic 2D Flash game engine: `http://flashpunk.net/`

Unity

A 3D game engine that runs on multiple platforms: http://unity3d.com/

Ren'Py

A python-based visual novel engine: http://www.renpy.org/

Game Maker

A tool that makes games on multiple platforms with minimal programming required: http://www.yoyogames.com/gamemaker/windows

Multimedia Fusion

Make PC games without needing to program:
http://www.clickteam.com/eng/mmf2.php

Corona SDK

A very popular commercial mobile app game engine:
http://www.anscamobile.com/corona/

haXe + NME

A completely free, open source cross-platform language and series of plugins which are very similar to AS3 (Flash ActionScript) but compile to native apps by translating your code into other languages, from C++ to JavaScript. One codebase can compile to a native, hardware accelerated game on Windows, Mac, iPhone, iPad, android phones and tablets, Flash and HTML5: http://www.haxenme.org/

CryEngine

A free (for non-commercial games) AAA quality 3D game engine that is gaining in popularity. An alternative to the **UDK (Unreal Development Kit)**:
http://mycryengine.com/

XNA

Microsoft's great 2D game making kit for PC and XBOX:
http://create.msdn.com/en-US/

BlitzMax

Program Windows, MacOS X, and Linux games in BASIC:
`http://www.blitzbasic.com/Products/_index_.php`

The Unreal Development Kit

UDK is the world-class AAA game engine as seen on consoles:
`http://www.udk.com/`

jMonkeyEngine

A high quality cross-platform Java openGL game engine:
`http://jmonkeyengine.com/`

Stencyl

Designed to make both Flash and iOS games with minimal coding:
`http://www.stencyl.com/`

Torque

A great cross-platform game engine with a large community:
`http://www.garagegames.com/`

Construct

Make multiplatform games with no programming required:
`http://www.scirra.com/`

HTML5 game engines aplenty

There are dozens of well-made HTML5 game engines online, such as:

- `http://impactjs.com/`
- `http://www.jawsjs.com`
- `http://www.limejs.com/`
- `http://www.kesiev.com/akihabara/`
- `http://easeljs.com/`

There are quite literally tens of thousands of game engines on the web, and listing them all here wouldn't be that useful. HTML5 is destined to be big in the future, but tried-and-tested mediums such as Flash remain very popular. There's always the "next big thing" to consider with regard to engine technology, so if you want to target consoles or mobile or 3D games using WebGL or Flash Stage3D (Molehill) you would do well to do a little Googling.

You don't even have to start with a game engine. If you are hardcore, love coding, or just want additional challenge it is entirely possible to start from scratch, creating your own game engine in the language of your choice.

Helpful Tools

Essential tools

The Internet is filled with helpful tools that can aid you in your quest to create a great game. One particularly great resource is "The Big List of Game Making Tools"

```
http://www.pixelprospector.com/the-big-list-of-game-making-tools/
```

Recording time-lapse videos

Many Game Jams encourage participants to create a **time-lapse video** of the process. It can be really interesting to see an entire weekend's work in fast forward. To do so, you can download a tool that takes screenshots every minute or so and then stitch them into a video for posting on Youtube or Vimeo. An example would be **Chronolapse** which was created by a veteran Ludum Dare game Jammer and is freeware open source for most platforms.

```
http://keeyai.com/projects-and-releases/chronolapse/
```

Chronolapse will do all the hard work for you – it can be set up to take screenshots of both your desktop and optionally (with picture-in-picture) your webcam, and once the weekend is over it will automatically turn this folder full of images into a video file.

Here are over 500 examples of Game Jam time-lapse videos:

```
http://www.youtube.com/results?search_type=videos&search_
query=ludum+dare+timelapse
```

Time-lapse videos are becoming a mainstay of the bigger Jams because they give a glimpse into the flurry of activity that each Jammer experiences during the weekend. They can be really funny, showing mistakes and work-in-progress, and they reveal the method each person took to make their game. Finally, anyone ever accused of not starting from scratch or submitting a previously-made game need only show a time-lapse of their efforts to prove their innocence.

IRC chat clients

Another essential tool during a Game Jam is an **IRC chat program** if you are participating in discussions with your fellow competitors. Many web clients exist to do this in your browser, or programs such as Pidgin come highly recommended because they are freeware open source and work on most platforms, but there are hundreds of IRC clients for you to choose from.

- `http://www.pidgin.im/`
- `http://www.silverex.org/`
- `http://www.mirc.com/`
- `http://chatzilla.hacksrus.com/`

Generating sound effects

Time and time again, one sound generator app comes up in Game Jam discussions as a great way to make retro sound effects. Written by a veteran game Jammer, **SFXR** and its many variants (it has been ported to C++, Flash, JavaScript and more) have been used in over 100 games. If you need 8-bit, old-school beeps, jumps, coin sounds or explosions, this is a great tool for making them. You can randomize the many controls or tweak to your heart's content and come up with a sound that nobody has ever heard before. Included is example source code which will allow your game to generate the sounds at runtime. This means that you do not need to bloat your game's download size with data files, instead generating them in RAM on demand using only a few bytes of data.

- Original Windows Version: `http://www.drpetter.se/project_sfxr.html`
- Mac Port: `http://mac.softpedia.com/get/Developer-Tools/cfxr.shtml`
- Linux Port: `http://n3wt0n.com/blog/drpetters-sfxr-with-ubuntu-810/`
- Flash AS3 Port: `http://www.superflashbros.net/as3sfxr/`

- Advanced Flex Version: `http://www.bfxr.net/`

Finally, one of the best resources for obtaining free (legal) sound effects and music is `http://www.freesound.org/`

Level editors

Man game Jammers end up programming their own home-brewed level editor (or even hard-code levels in their sources by using an array in the code) but there are some very popular level design tools that are mentioned again and again. These tools typically output either source code or .XML data for tile-based level geometry and can be a great resource for fleshing out your game world.

OGMO

`http://ogmoeditor.com/`

DAME

`http://dambots.com/dame-editor/`

GLEED

`http://gleed2d.codeplex.com/`

MapEditor

`http://www.mapeditor.org/`

Mappy

`http://tilemap.co.uk/mappy.php`

TME - Tile Map Editor

`http://tilemapeditor.com/`

TileStudio

`http://tilestudio.sourceforge.net/`

tIDE (Tilemap Integrated Development Environment)

`http://tide.codeplex.com/`

The Community

Social networking links

Here are a few essential networking opportunities with massive Game Jamming communities.

Google+

```
https://plus.google.com/
```

Perhaps it is because the technology is brand new, but Google+ is filled with game developers. Gamedevs share code, war stories, screenshots, videos, and links to their games, and the conversation regarding tools, languages, and algorithms is very active. You're missing out if you don't circle a few dozen game developers here.

To start you out, here are a few people involved in the community who are well worth following:

- **Mike Kasprzak** (organizer of Ludum Dare)

  ```
  https://plus.google.com/104742881147390208350
  ```

- **Phil Hassey** (organizer of Ludum Dare)

  ```
  https://plus.google.com/115283698152321681798
  ```

- **Mike Hommel** (organizer of Ludum Dare)

  ```
  https://plus.google.com/101713959382687203463
  ```

- **Pekka Kujansuu** (Ludum Dare admin)

  ```
  https://plus.google.com/108792302762385685386
  ```

- **Chevy Johnston** (creator of *Flashpunk* and 2x Ludum Dare Winner)
  https://plus.google.com/103872388664329802170

- **Sophie Houlden** (frequent Game Jammer)
  https://plus.google.com/107041886896411603117

- **Adam Saltsman** (creator of *Flixel*)
  https://plus.google.com/112979675666832878058

- **Mike Acton** (curator of aldevblogaday)
  https://plus.google.com/105595823502776413734

- **Christer Kaitila** (the author of this book)
  https://plus.google.com/101390729659078829753

In addition, you should follow these Google+ business pages:

- **GameJamming** (news about upcoming Game Jams)
  https://plus.google.com/109613269982984742720

- **Ludum Dare** (news about all things LD48)
  https://plus.google.com/102365835308117936555

- **IGDA Global Game Jam** (news about the GGJ)
  https://plus.google.com/102068346576091895888

Twitter

The best way to make use of Twitter for Game Jam networking is by using the right hashtags.

For example, every Saturday, game developers post screenshots of their work in progress by including the tag **#screenshotsaturday** so that others looking for the same kind of post will be able to find them. A popular website, www.screenshotsaturday.com scans Twitter for you and collects all these fantastic images into a gallery that you don't want to miss. The best way to find other game developers to follow is by clicking the usernames of people who post using this hashtag. With around 100 screenshots posted every week, you will find this a great source of inspiration.

Gamedev images from Twitter

Another Twitter hashtag to search for is `#LD48` (the Ludum Dare tag) and `#ggj` (during the time of year when the Global Game Jam is on) and equivalent yearly tags (`#ggj11`, `#ggj12`, and so on). Generic hashtag that frequently come up are `#gamejam` and `#gamedev`.

Search for the term "Game Jam" to find others using this link:
`http://Twitter.com/#!/search/game%20jam`.

IRC chat rooms aplenty

There are many IRC chat rooms devoted to Game Jamming.
The most popular is: `#ludumdare` on IRC.afternet.org
(`https://qwebirc.afternet.org/?channels=LudumDare`).

Reddit

`http://www.reddit.com/r/gamedev`

A massive forum listing with tons of game developers. Search for additional threads such as `/r/bacongamejam/` and `r/redditgamejam/` and `/r/indiegaming/`.

TIGforums

`http://forums.tigsource.com/`

With over 500,000 forum posts, these forums are probably the most active game development forums around. Well worth participating. There are topics devoted to Game Jamming, and many new Jams are first announced here.

Other websites worth visiting

The calendar of upcoming Game Jams at `http://www.compohub.net` can be a great way to find your next Jam. The blog `http://www.gamejamming.com` also includes a calendar of events as well as articles cross-posted from its Google+ account.

Other very important game development websites that often contain information regarding Game Jams include `http://www.DIYgames.com`, `http://www.modDB.com`, `http://www.indieDB.com`, `http://www.devmaster.net`, `http://www.gamedev.net`, `http://www.dcemu.co.uk`, `http://www.tigsource.com`, `http://www.gamasutra.com`, and `http://www.videogamecoder.com` just to name a few.

Finally, many of the Jams themselves, such as `http://www.ludumdare.com/compo/`, `http://www.experimentalgameplay.com`, and `http://www.superfriendshipclub.com/forum/` have highly active user forums or blogs that are well worth checking out in order to connect with others in the community.

Afterword

A note from the author

Thank you very much for reading this book. It was inspiring talking to so many people about Game Jams—I learned a lot and made a few new friends in the process.

My hope is that the effort that went into writing it was worthwhile. If you learned something, had a little fun, or simply satisfied some of your curiosity, my mission has been accomplished.

I'd like to sincerely thank the following people who I interviewed for the book: Ian Schreiber, Jason P. Kaplan, Austin Breed, Christopher Nilssen, Mike Kasprzak, Chevy Ray Johnston, Pekka Kujansuu, Phil Hassey, Chris Hopp, Zuraida Buter, Mike Hommel, Foaad Khosmood, Eric McQuiggan, and Dr. Mike Reddy. Many more were kind enough to e-mail me poems, ideas, and advice, and I am grateful for those contributions as well. They aren't all listed here but their efforts are appreciated.

Be sure to check out `http://www.mcfunkypants.com` which is my personal blog, where you will find all sorts of games to play, source code to download, addenda and errata, and much more. You are warmly encouraged to follow me on Twitter: `http://Twitter.com/McFunkypants` and Google+: `http://mcfunkypants.com/+/`.

Hearing from you would make my day, so please feel welcome to reach out. If you make a cool new game in a Game Jam and would like to show it to me, please do. I'd love to hear about the games you make!

Sincerely,

Christer Kaitila
(a.k.a. Breakdance McFunkypants)

Index

H

hand-crafted
versus computer generated content 48
haXe + NME
URL 80
headaches
avoiding 52, 53
HTML5 game engines
URL 81, 82
Humble Indie Bundle
URL 71

I

Ian Schreiber, expert talk
about 24
blog, URL 24
twitter, URL 24
IGDA Global Game Jam
Google+ business page, URL 88
Indiecity
URL 71
IRC chat program
about 84
IRC clients, URL 84
IRC chat rooms 89

J

Jason P. Kaplan, expert talk
about 13, 14
game Jam, URL 14
twitter, URL 14
website, URL 14
jMonkeyEngine
URL 81

K

Keep It Simple, Stupid!. *See* **K.I.S.S Rule**
K.I.S.S. Rule 42, 43
Klik of the Month Klub
URL 77

L

level editors

DAME 85
GLEED 85
MapEditor 85
Mappy 85
OGMO 85
tIDE 85
TileStudio 85
TME 85
Ludum Dare
Google+ business page, URL 88
survey stats 12, 13
URL 76
Ludum Dare 19
winner, URL 56

M

MapEditor
URL 85
Mappy
URL 85
Markus Persson (Notch) 71
Mike Acton, expert talk
Google+, URL 88
Mike Hommel, expert talk
about 22
Google+, URL 22, 87
twitter, URL 22
website, URL 22
Mike Kasprzak, expert talk
about 16
blog, URL 16
Google+, URL 16, 87
twitter, URL 16
motivation techniques
about 38
the wall, getting over 38
work-in progress, showing 38
Multimedia Fusion
URL 80
mythical man-month
URL 46

N

name, Game Jam
importance 60

[PACKT] Thank you for buying
PUBLISHING
The Game Jam Survival Guide

About Packt Publishing

Packt, pronounced 'packed', published its first book "*Mastering phpMyAdmin for Effective MySQL Management*" in April 2004 and subsequently continued to specialize in publishing highly focused books on specific technologies and solutions.

Our books and publications share the experiences of your fellow IT professionals in adapting and customizing today's systems, applications, and frameworks. Our solution based books give you the knowledge and power to customize the software and technologies you're using to get the job done. Packt books are more specific and less general than the IT books you have seen in the past. Our unique business model allows us to bring you more focused information, giving you more of what you need to know, and less of what you don't.

Packt is a modern, yet unique publishing company, which focuses on producing quality, cutting-edge books for communities of developers, administrators, and newbies alike. For more information, please visit our website: www.packtpub.com.

Writing for Packt

We welcome all inquiries from people who are interested in authoring. Book proposals should be sent to author@packtpub.com. If your book idea is still at an early stage and you would like to discuss it first before writing a formal book proposal, contact us; one of our commissioning editors will get in touch with you.

We're not just looking for published authors; if you have strong technical skills but no writing experience, our experienced editors can help you develop a writing career, or simply get some additional reward for your expertise.

Corona SDK Mobile Game Development: Beginner's Guide

ISBN: 978-1-84969-188-8   Paperback: 350 pages

Create monetized games for iOS and Andriod with minimum cost and code

1. Build once and deploy your games to both iOS and Android

2. Create commercially successful games by applying several monetization techniques and tools

3. Create three fun games and integrate them with social networks such as Twitter and Facebook

CryENGINE 3 Cookbook

ISBN: 978-1-84969-106-2   Paperback: 324 pages

Over 90 recipes written by Crytek developers for creating third-generation real-time games

1. Begin developing your AAA game or simulation by harnessing the power of the award winning CryENGINE3

2. Create entire game worlds using the powerful CryENGINE 3 Sandbox.

3. Create your very own customized content for use within the CryENGINE3 with the multiple creation recipes in this book

4. Translate your design into CryENGINE by following the easy step by step recipes exploring flow graph, track view, and many of the other tools within CryENGINE

Please check **www.PacktPub.com** for information on our titles

Unity 3.x Game Development by Example Beginner's Guide

ISBN: 978-1-84969-184-0   Paperback: 408 pages

A seat-of-your-pants manual for building fun, groovy little games quickly with Unity 3.x

1. Build fun games using the free Unity game engine even if you've never coded before

2. Learn how to "skin" projects to make totally different games from the same file – more games, less effort!

3. Deploy your games to the Internet so that your friends and family can play them

4. Packed with ideas, inspiration, and advice for your own game design and development

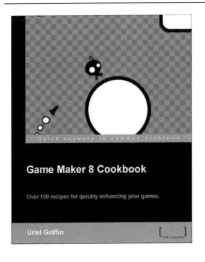

Game Maker 8 Cookbook

ISBN: 978-1-84969-062-1   Paperback: 346 pages

Over 100 recipes for quickly enhancing your games

1. Enhance the complexity of your games using the Game Maker Language.

2. Apply these recipes to virtually any type of game, including 3D and online games!

3. Simple, well explained recipes designed for game maker enthusiasts at all levels.

Please check **www.PacktPub.com** for information on our titles

Printed in Great Britain
by Amazon